DIAMOND HEDGE PRODUCTIONS, LLC

Discerning Spirits

Visionary Gifts in Practice

Alexandra Clair

Author of Wood's End, e-book on Screw Pulp, Kindle, and Nook. Soft cover at Amazon

Thank you to Paul Mayer, a gifted editor, and to Brian Churchill both valued friends. Cover design by Brian Churchill / Churchill Studios, Memphis, TN

ISBN: 978-0-9847059-0-0 / Copyright May 2013

CHAPTER ONE

THE SEEN AND THE UNSEEN

...while we look not at the things which are seen, but at the things which are not seen; for the things which are seen are temporal, but the things which are not seen are eternal (2ⁿᵈ Corinthians 4: 18).

For those that keep reading some of this may seem almost improper to discuss. For too many in the church exploring the supernatural is taboo. For others, this book will confirm what they already experience in the practice of a deliverance ministry and provide an enhanced framework and common language that allows us to share in the advancement of a Christian response.

I am writing about a dark subject but, hopefully I am addressing believers who know their unassailable, victorious position in Christ as sons and daughters of the Most High King. This book presupposes that my readers are Christians.

"Discerning Spirits" is the number one phrase that gets people to my blog. www.alexandraclair.com It is also the subject that draws people to email me, telling of their own experiences, asking questions, and sharing concerns.

This book is for you.

Discernment allows us to arrive at conclusions that can't be quantified or explained without acknowledging that... *all things came into being through Him, and apart from Him nothing came into being that has come into being (John 1: 3).* God created everything in the universe – the material and the immaterial – this world and all that lay beyond, parallel and within, beneath and above, known and unknown, seen and unseen. Jesus did not leave us as orphans (*John 14: 18*). Through His word we are provided rich instruction to minister light in dark strongholds of bondage.

It's said that knowledge is acquired, but that wisdom is given. Discernment makes spiritual insight possible. We have the five senses of sight, hearing, taste, touch, and smell. But there is a whole host of other senses that inform spiritual perception.

Discerning spirits is the gift of seeing with the "eyes of the heart" into the unseen dimensions to prepare us for battle. Like the visionary gift of prophecy it is settled deep in the creative core of who God designed us to be long before we were born. Since discerning spirits is present from birth, like perfect pitch or an aptitude for numbers, many who have this ability are uneasy with and remain silent or secretive. Though the gift itself may be little understood, some are compelled by God to embark on a journey that draws them to the use of this gift as a ministry of Christ.

Proper use and understanding of discerning spirits is evidence of a mature Christian, enabling the senses to see the truth beneath the veneer, the unseen demonic imprint. ***But solid food is for the mature, who because of practice have their senses trained to discern good and evil (Hebrews 5: 14).***

All visionary gifts are empowered by a true faith. Proof of legitimacy is that each is paired with discernment. Discernment manifests when partnered with another gift and allows us to judge something as being true or false, good or evil. Examples are:

- Discernment/Discerning Spirits
- Discernment/Healing
- Discernment/Prophecy
- Discernment/Deliverance
- Discernment/Intercession
- Discernment/Evangelism

A visionary gift is intended by design and purpose to operate in a particular supernatural context against the enemy. While all spiritual gifts are supernaturally imparted, some have a battle purpose and design that others do not.

Deliverance suggests a broad range of applications. It is freedom (deliverance) from evil spirits and demons; a literal transfer from darkness to light and also supernatural extrication, destruction of, or cleansing from one or all of the three occult "i-centered strongholds." These "i-strongholds" are:

- Imprint
- Infestation
- Influence

I use these words as a classification tool when I investigate a place or situation. They help identify the kind of strongholds that need to be dismantled, cleansed, or destroyed. These words have a specific scope of meaning and will be referred to throughout the content of this book. When I use the word PRETERNATURAL I'm primarily speaking to evidence of satan manifesting through imprint, infestation, and influence. When I use the word SUPERNATURAL, I'm alluding to a miracle or unseen manifestation of how God and angels impact our life on planet earth. We see the distinction.

4

Satanic-Imprint is a stamp, a kind of literal tattoo that announces to the world that something belongs to satan. As is the case with every evil practice and principle, we see a perverse inversion or mimicking of what is Godly. The satanic imprint mimics the "seal of the righteousness of faith" that identifies all believers as belonging to Jesus Christ. ***Nevertheless, the firm foundation of God stands, having this seal, "The Lord knows those who are His," and, "Everyone who names the name of the Lord is to abstain from wickedness" (2nd Timothy 2: 19a).***

The satanic imprint, or character, is an embedded, "hands off" message that conveys deceit, fear, and intimidation. It is the bluster that dissuades the Christian from suiting up (***Ephesians 6: 10-24***) and stepping forward. Those who have a developed ability to discern spirits interpret a satanic-imprint as a heaviness that alerts us to a need for battle-ready status. This is what intercessors mean when they say, "breaking through." In prayer they are made aware of these imprints around which barriers of evil protection exist. Many intercessors have a strong gift of mercy which empathetically communicates what the deliverance team needs to know.

What I tend to experience as my first clue is a degree of confusion. There is a certain disconnect between what is apparent and what is real. This presents as an actual energy field of preternatural blindness intended to dissuade investigation and discourage prayer. It's like you've walked onto a theatrical set only you don't fully recognize it as such. There's food on the table. You are hungry and everything looks great. You can almost smell the aroma and might even reach out to pick up an apple, a turkey leg, a turnover. But... this stuff is not real and if you consumed any of it your health would be compromised. Every bit is molded plastic, a perfectly presented decoy; strategy, imprint, dissemination.

Satan claims legal access to this world because of humanity's sin and defends his territory; often by hiding. The satanic imprint foreshadows the mark of the beast in Revelation. Though some want to imagine this mark as being present only during a certain period of coming history, like all such patterns of practice which denote where allegiances lie, the mark of the beast is with us today in shadow; less evident, but nevertheless, present. ***And the smoke of their torment goes up forever and ever; they have no rest day and night, those who worship the beast and his image, and whoever receives the mark of his name (Revelation: 14: 11)***

As the imprint drives the image into flesh there is an exchange that takes place. The degree of this evil imprint is the degree to which the battle is framed. This imprint informs the ways that a deliverance team partners with saints that have the spiritual gift of healing. Healing is part of the aftercare process, but via faith is also needed during the actual deliverance.

A stamp can be washed off. A seal has an official, even a royal, connotation. The Father's seal carries authority of the highest order and will permanently destroy the satanic imprint. ***Do not work for the food which perishes, but for the food which endures to eternal life, which the Son of Man will give to you, for on Him the father, God, has set His seal (John 6: 27).***

Every believer has a divine calling and God's holy seal denoting the righteousness of a true faith. This seal affirms the light we carry and clearly identifies us as Holy Spirit-carriers. ***The light shines in the darkness and the darkness did not comprehend it (John 1: 5).***

I like to envision this when I step into deliverance or any other difficult situation. I imagine the seal blazing forth from my forehead as a warning to every demon or evil spirit in my path. I also imagine God's hand holding mine. Paul made a connection between the royal seal as the proof (outcome) of his calling when he wrote... ***for you are the seal of my apostleship in the Lord (1st Corinthians 9: 2b).***

An evil imprint may be discerned by believers long before hard evidence reveals it. The satanic imprint drives the decisions and infects the policies of individuals or systems that bear it. My friend, Brenda, was asked to serve on the board of directors of a Christian ministry. After several meetings she discerned that the board was spiritually unhealthy and reflected the toxic character of the executive director. Because of this compromise of leadership, a lack of accountability, and failure to investigate beyond the superficial, the staff suffered satanic opposition in their various gifts and calling being used as God designed.

Brenda had no proof of this situation other than the sense of this unsettling imprint which God disclosed to her; that, coupled with her critical thinking skills fostered suspicions which the Holy Spirit confirmed as she prayed. She resigned. Two years later a scandal revealed the degree to which God had been abandoned in the policies and practices of this ministry.

Pay attention to your instincts which draw you to recognize a satanic imprint. God is calling you to explore beyond the rhetoric and superficial appearance to discern the core of truth according to His statutes and Word, and to recognize the satanic imprint. The demonic imprint (pressed in demonic character) which pervasively imbues the illegal sale of drugs is a good example. Less obvious satanic imprints exist in facets of the unhealthy and toxic strongholds of religion and politics or even certain generational family dynamics.

God uses a person with the gift of discerning spirits to identify these imprints, and to direct the intercession, investigation, needed change, and next steps in deliverance. People who are intercessors are often the first to point out an evil imprint. They begin praying in preparation for deliverance and often wake in the night to pray with fresh knowledge having received a divine understanding that was previously concealed.

When God sends you into battle, you can count on the fact that brothers and sisters whom you don't know have been raised up to pray. Some of these intercessor-activists may have passed on to glory, but their prayers live on as a vibrant, supernatural force which never dies.

Infestations exist where demon entities and unclean spirits congregate. They are given legal access via sin; additionally through pagan practice, ritual, worship or by direct invitation. An example is a haunted property where manifestations of evil spirits harass people. Infestations manifest in persons or things per satanic assignment.

The more dangerous situation is where demons enter and possess a human being. ***And He was asking him, "What is your name?" And he said to Him, "My name is Legion; for we are many" (Mark 5: 9).*** Jesus did not need to ask this question. He already knew the answer. Jesus is offering a practical teaching as He shows us something about the practice of exorcism to equip us so that we can follow His example of stepping into such a battle.

Infestations are clusters of demonic attachments which imbue unholy areas of politics, commerce, or religion. Often the failure of society to hold perpetrators legally accountable open doors for demonic infestations to grow around enterprises motivated by greed, power, or lust.

Influence is the introduction of suggestive patterns of thought into individual minds, and/or, the societal general consciousness. Demonic influence takes on form when the church (body of Christ) is slow to respond. Or, even worse, when the church is entirely unengaged leaving a vacuum from which demonic infestations launch an assault in order to gain influence in the form of a stronghold. The stronghold reflects the character and sphere of influence. We can view this in the micro or macro context.

The counter to such influence is choice. I think of choice as a muscle. As we apply deductive reasoning in the light of scripture and exercise moral choices the gift of wisdom becomes operational and repels evil.

Choice is the godly attribute that sets us apart. Life requires us to continually make decisions. These decisions form a personal sphere of influence for good or ill. Too many people end up playing the role of passive facilitator, inadvertently partnering with evil in a failure to act. Wherever satan is active we recognize that in some way choice has been strategically disabled. If as children we were continually criticized we may be fearful of exercising choice as a godly imperative. We see choice disabled in all unhealthy relationships, in life consuming addictions, in cults, in certain political structures... the list is endless.

Our choices define our character, and our character determines our influence. People are either drawn to us or repelled by this influence. We want our behavior to reflect Christ. David expressed this commitment in Psalm 101. ***Morning by morning I will destroy all the wicked in the land, cutting off all evildoers from the city of the Lord (Psalm 101: 8).*** Jesus said, ***"If you love Me you will keep my commandments" (John 14: 15).***

The legalistic adherence to a form of faith isn't real. We recognize that without Christ we are powerless and He is sovereign; consigning our choices and our actions to His camp of influence. ***Not everyone who says to me, 'Lord, Lord," will enter the kingdom of heaven, but he who does the will of My Father who is in heaven <u>will enter</u> (Matthew 7: 21).***

Obedience in the quantitative substance of choice is far more than intellectual agreement. If our faith is not obvious to those around us in this embattled world, it may be time for a period of reflection and self examination. It may be time to pause and reconnoiter, make a military observation. Obedience is the privileged, risk-taking adherence to choices that transcend circumstances. By it we embrace a code of ethics. ***Many will say to Me on that day, 'Lord, Lord, did we not prophecy in Your name, and in Your name cast out demons, and in Your name perform many miracles?' And then I will declare to them, 'I never knew you; depart from Me, you who practice lawlessness (Matthew 7: 22, 23).***

The same principles are true of demonic influence. Before the fall, satan was a cherub, the chief worship/music leader and a persuasive communicator. Satan disguises himself as an angel of light because it formerly was an angel of light (***2nd Corinthians 11: 14***). Many cherubs, particularly gifted in the creative arts, fell with satan during the war in heaven. Other demons are warriors or may be assigned to harmful carrier elements which cause physical disease. Others imbue politics and religion. Some are heads of satanic principalities and territories. What all have in common is that they are now utterly perverted and eternally damned to hell.

In discerning the spirits within the stronghold of influence we look at what the objective seems to be in any given circumstance and this sheds light on how we should proceed. Where people are concerned temptations revolve around greed, lust, or power. Where satan is concerned we do battle against the death goal or other outcome attached to that battle. (***Ezekiel 28: 11-19; Revelation 12: 7-12; Isaiah 14: 10-27***)

Much of the way that satan establishes "influence" are tied to how God created this fallen spirit-being in the original role of a cherub-angel. Satan hijacks the inventive, creative process for an evil agenda. It is ironic that choice, which facilitates creativity, is the very element satan most hates. It is a mistake to point to a vehicle like social media and pronounce it evil. Technology may be a conduit for evil, but is just as effectively an overwhelming force for good. We never want to "throw the baby out with the bath water." In rejecting the supernatural many denominations have unintentionally partnered with satan in doing this.

There is a reason why satan is called the prince of the power of the air. (***Daniel 8: 25; John 16: 11; Eph 2: 2***) Satan's influence moves into our seen-realm through unseen dimensions as concepts, temptations, thoughts, and occult knowledge. None of this has a material form unless the satanic agenda partners with human conduits via the exercise of human will and choice as evidenced by behavior. Today satanic actions manifest through humans in attempts at misinformation, inaccurate or fluff media reporting, and blatant thought control. These efforts are highly sophisticated in disabling critical thinking skills and form an evil, strategic communications agenda as we move toward prophetic events described in scripture.

Not every thought we have is ours. (***1st John 4: 1; 2nd Corinthians 10: 5***) In our modern technological age we are subjected to many attempts at sophisticated mind control. All cults - and all those that are blatantly satanic - use mind control in order to disable choice, to keep victims from escaping such bondage and reporting the crimes committed against them.

Healthy people ask for what they need. They make healthy requests of those around them and in prayer to Christ... ***in whom we have boldness and confident access through faith in Him (Ephesians 3: 12).*** They ask for what they need in the will of God as described in James chapter four. In part... ***you do not have because you do not ask (James 4: 2c).*** When we interview people about their need for deliverance we want to understand the degree to which choice has been limited by trauma, assault, intimidation, and fear. When we make these connections we learn about the strongholds. This, in turn, informs deliverance. This also determines the kind of aftercare that is offered since faith and confidence in exercising the new freedom in Christ needs to be nourished and reinforced.

Satanic influence reinforces a satanic agenda. Tolerance for violent video games and the subsequent life fallout and occult driven children's stories are obvious examples of how we pass on satanic influence to the next generation. This opens the door to evil influence moving into the realm of practice, which if uninterrupted, becomes a cursed stronghold from which people, including those who claim Christ as Savior, need deliverance.

Satanic influence is the slime laden assault that disables critical thinking, independence, and autonomy. The thing about slime is that it sticks. Then it spreads micro-toxins into the flesh. An example is a pornography dalliance that grows into an addiction, destroys a marriage, and leads to risky behaviors followed by physical disease. Influence can also apply to a confluence of circumstances that makes a wrong choice attractive. Many parents today need to confess the sin of failing to protect their children from occult assault.

More than temptation, demonic influence has a strategy which is filtered through an organized and diverse army of evil spirits and demons. Their sphere of influence is personally assaultive. It is societal, political, cultural and/or relational. By measured degree, as tolerance builds and rationalization kicks in, the satanic imprint draws men and women to partner with evil to greater degrees. This is the state of all unsaved humanity even though there was, a once shining time in the glow of innocence and idealism that this person may have determined to be "different."

It is impossible to escape the absorptive character of satanic influence without Jesus Christ as the indwelling power that overcomes. *For He rescued us from the domain of darkness, and transferred us to the kingdom of His beloved Son, in whom we have redemption, the forgiveness of sins (Colossians 1: 13)*

The kind of influence I'm talking about is given preternaturally charged mobility to strategically move beyond the entry point (initial sin) to gain ever wider access. In the interview (investigative phase) prior to deliverance we want to understand something about the influence that has, via human choice, become practice. We could be looking at a person or an organization, the micro and the macro with all the same basic principles and application. Practice which set up patterns (strongholds), which then become embedded behavioral addictions and or organizational cultures (domains), will lead to a soul, a body, a place, or a Christian labeled organization in desperate need of deliverance.

Begin now to pray that God's Holy Spirit will fine-tune your senses to recognize the imprint, discern the character of the infestation, and supernaturally guide your prayers to release the power of God in decimating the stronghold of influence. To this you are the "called of the Lord."

As a Holy Spirit carrier you stand in the divine light and freedom of Jesus Christ. Begin living in the literal power of what God reveals through His word. ***But thanks be to God in Christ who always leads us in triumph in Christ, and manifests through us the sweet aroma of the knowledge of Him in every place. For we are a fragrance of Christ to God among those who are being saved and among those who are perishing; to the one an aroma of death to death, to the other an aroma from life to life (2nd Corinthians 2: 14-16).***

CHAPTER TWO

HIJACKED AND HOODWINCKED

I will build my church; and the gates of Hades will not overcome it (Matthew 16: 18b).

We are now going to take a broad-brush look at two categories of the unsaved. In the next chapter we'll look at three categories of demon possession. All five loosely comprise the Christ-less, unsaved of the world.

Not to be included in any of the five categories I describe in this book are the mentally ill. Neither do we include those seriously impaired individuals; prevented from self determining a course of action through no fault of their own and cannot, in any way be clinically confused with psychopaths. In a politically correct culture we easily assign the false label of mental illness when some may be prime candidates for demonic attachment or enmeshment. We will later consider narcissism from a scriptural perspective.

God met us right where we were and a miracle of His grace transformed our lives. Below is verse three from the song, *Love of God*, said to have been written on the wall of an insane asylum by a mentally ill inmate over 100 years ago.

> Could we with ink the ocean fill,
> And were the skies of parchment made,
> Were every stalk on earth a quill,
> And every man a scribe by trade;
> To write the love of God above
> Would drain the ocean dry;
> Nor could the scroll contain the whole,
> Though stretched from sky to sky.

After we look at the first two categories in this chapter we will then consider three states of actual demon possession. There are many people who have a bias against the label, "exorcism." In service to how I understand this I use both terms. If you've allowed a denominational bias to steal a word that fits a broad designation time to decide you will grow beyond being manipulated in this way. Think! How does stripping a community of thought of a legitimate word-concept cripple critical discussions? ***Remind them of these things, and solemnly charge them in the presence of God*** *not to wrangle about words, which is useless and leads to the ruin of the hearers (2nd Timothy 2: 14)*

Let's be kind in understanding one another, because in most cases, though Christians may denominationally assign different words, once we've talked and shared, we realize that we can fundamentally agree.

We will also see how deliverance and exorcism more often than not overlap just as freedom from evil spirits is also healing from the trauma left in the wake of such bondage and additionally brings physical healing. Understanding this confluence lends depth and informs our prayer life even as it allows us to formulate an effective response that is battle ready in accordance with His equipping glory.

Jesus twice makes the following point: ***And I give eternal life to them, and they will never perish; and <u>no one will snatch them out of My hand.</u> My Father, who has given them to Me, is greater than all; <u>and no one is able to snatch them out of the Father's hand.</u> I and the Father are one" (John 10: 28-30).*** As a foundation to what follows read ***Romans 1: 18-32***.

The first believers lived in very harsh and dangerous times in an occupied land where the Romans had been brutally at war with the native Israelite population for generations. In this environment it wasn't all that difficult to identify the enemy. There was a lethal imbalance of power, alien troops with brutal despot leaders having control over livelihood and fate. To any that politically rebelled judgment was swift and final. The Hebrew religious authority walked a fine political line as go betweens. The people had been without a Prophet for 500 years and its leaders, the Pharisees and scribes, had succumbed to the pagan influence and infestation of a pagan societal imprint. Healthy human response had devolved into a spirit of fear based accommodation. Such times bring into sharp relief what is less evident in more civil epochs of history.

It is from the dynamics of this perilous history that Paul, inspired by the Holy Spirit, paints a vivid word picture of the unsaved in ***Romans 1: 18-32***. After reading these passages can we agree that a righteous and sovereign God has every right to judge His creation? Bottom line... we cannot have God on our terms and must accept that what Paul writes is true. Untold numbers of people will never see heaven and will be consigned to hell. Their demonically co-opted and hijacked lives set up strongholds of influence from which deliverance is needed. Father God who said so is... ***The Rock! His work is perfect, for all His ways are just; A God of faithfulness, and without*** *injustice. **Righteous and upright is He (Deuteronomy 32: 4).***

Paul provided further insight when he wrote 1ˢᵗ Corinthians chapter five. Here we see a sharp and clear delineation in response in how we judge one another in the body of Christ and how we view those outside the body of Christ who are unsaved.

I write more about this later, but it is an absolute mandate and necessity that we hold our brothers and sisters in Christ accountable for sin. Although some like to focus on the unsaved masses, because comparatively speaking they appear to be in worse shape, the fact is that we are not to waste our precious time judging those who don't have Christ.

Why is this, the case?   Because the lost are already under a sentence of divine condemnation and as a norm of genuine faith we should have already worked out a response. This response may look a little different for each person, but in the confluence of who God created us to be, our life commitments would flow out of a spiritual gift set, sphere of influence, and divine calling. We would have decided to partner with God for godly purposes via choice and decision.

Having a Holy Spirit inspired compassion for the lost we feel empathy. The "redeemed of the Lord" are empowered to extend the light of love, even boundary laden love which crosses the deep divides of unseen opposition to reach those in desperate longing for the Creator of the universe. ***Romans 1: 18-32***, clearly lays out the truth. We can't be effective in areas we don't acknowledge and since it is so politically incorrect to say that many people will die without Christ and will be condemned to hell (a real place) genuine Holy Spirit empowered gifts of evangelism are smothered. It is this empathy and desire to see people free from sin and living in the joy of fellowship with Jesus Christ that moves us to minister in dark places. To this end the apostle Paul, the great evangelist wrote:

***I wrote to you in my letter not to associate with immoral people; I did not at all mean with the immoral people of this world, or with the covetous and swindlers, or with the idolaters, for then you would have to go out of the world (1ˢᵗ Corinthians 5: 9, 10).* Read the entire chapter.**

The unsaved, those who lack faith in Jesus Christ, fall into two very broad categories.
- The Unconsciously Oppressed
- The Willingly Influenced

1. **The Unconsciously Oppressed**, impaired by original sin, are additionally preternaturally blinded. They are the unsaved

masses that experience the consequence of sin and search for answers and a way to fill the void of life without Jesus Christ. These people are acutely aware when they cross a line to sin, but may be oblivious to the deeper need for the Savior. They know right from wrong and are capable of living a moral life. Most learn from their mistakes and seek to improve the quality of their lives by abstaining from what they consider to be unhealthy.

Some may have openly rebelled against convention, but retain a strong sense of justice with a genuine desire for fairness and equity, even when that fairness is unconventionally manifested. These people can do much good, but without Jesus Christ they will die and go to hell.

The unconsciously oppressed do not belong to Jesus Christ. Many genuinely adopt the Christian perspective which they implement as a kind of philosophy. Some may attend services and believe they are saved because the salt-less institution tells them they are. They are preternaturally deluded and duped into accepting the hypocritical form of religion whatever that happens to be. They walk out usually structured and legalistic principals with misguided passion which spills over into systems, cultures, and traditions which seek to subvert the loving and forgiving character of Jesus Christ.

Others attach to a substitute spiritual fulfillment that massages the satanic imprint of a self-constructed belief system. In many cultures they may ardently pursue an alternate religion. These people would not claim to be atheists. Really there are no atheists. All people believe in something even if that is merely a grandiose conception of self. *For since the creation of the world His invisible attributes, His eternal power and divine nature, have been clearly seen, being understood through what has been made, so that they are without excuse (Romans 1: 20).*

We are told in scripture to guard ourselves from idols. This is because in the worship of idols demons gather and become the power behind that idol, whatever it happens to be. Judging the lost little by little God gives each person every opportunity to repent. *Behold, I stand at the door and knock; if anyone hears My voice and opens the door, I will come in to him and will dine with him, and he with Me (Revelation 3: 20).*

I was recently at a dinner party. The subject of the Mayan calendar and the end of the world came up. One of the guests shared that he had visited the Mayan ruins and at the suggestion of the tour guide had placed his hand on a wall and made a wish in imitation of a pagan rite. What he wished for later came true. He twice stated, "I've never told anyone what that wish was and I never will, but it did come true." I couldn't let the second comment pass. I made mention of the powerful occult imprint that would have lingered in that place where so much human sacrifice and violence had taken place. I could literally feel the evil spirit bristle for, implicit in my comments, was criticism.

"When he prays about possessions and his marriage and children, he is not ashamed to address a lifeless thing. For health he appeals to a thing that is weak; for life he prays to a thing that is dead; for aid he entreats a thing that is utterly inexperienced; for a prosperous journey, a thing that cannot take a step; for money-making and work and success with his hands he asks strength of a thing whose hands have no strength" *(Wisdom of Solomon: 13: 17-19.) Also Psalm 115: 2-8.*

When using the word, pagan, some imagine that isolated tribe in the middle of nowhere. But pagan influences have been sophisticated and advanced and are with us at every stratum of culture and society. In the verses above we see that pagan cultures have lifted up idols behind which demonic cadre's of infestation gather as at a launching point, awaiting battle instructions and open doors via human invitation. From the evil power of such thrones they attach, maneuver, and manipulate the well meaning intentions of sincere people.

In deliverance of place we always find items dedicated to demons. These could be unchristian images, pagan artifacts and occult tools, an antique imbued by spiritist activity or some other satanically utilized or dedicated thing. Drug and pornography paraphernalia fall into this category as do some books such as the Sixth and Seventh Book of Moses. We also see that evil spirit entities, fixated in the last waning energy fields of sin and death, remain under specific assignment in certain places. They might like to leave, but without another human conduit they are stuck until a blinded and sinful narcissist, a curious dupe, or a practicing occultist arrives on the scene. Desperate and overplaying their hand, some unholy spirits make their presence known in these haunted places. Other demons are far more malevolent and cunning in the seduction of human beings.

2. **The Willingly Influenced** are invested in the lie that what they feel entitled to comprise a reality of their own making. Playing God they are influenced by demonic, preternatural infestations to which they willingly attach and partner.

In successfully constructing a façade they evidence some narcissistic traits. They have crippled the internal braking system which would allow them to take a hard look at their commitments.

Here we see how God intervenes through circumstances and at such junctures of extreme angst, depression, or forced reckoning God sends His children to minister the love of Christ.

A person I once worked with came to Christ from such a background. He had been raised in a family that made their living from the drug trade. When he brought his fiancé home to meet some of his family years later they were convinced she was an undercover FBI agent. When he first entered prison two of his brothers were already there. After decades of getting away with crime another was arrested with a cousin in South America. Only one brother seemed to have escaped, joining the military and putting distance between himself and his family after graduating high school.

Isolated for an episode of violence a guard began to share Christ with this man. On his last night, before returning to general population, he turned his life over to the Savior of the universe, Jesus Christ. I will always remember him saying that God began by miraculously taking away certain sinful desires so that he could stand and walk in the power of a new faith. But then began the path to walking out the gift of divine transformation; born anew. There were setbacks and mistakes. There were also well meaning Christians who, enamored of a dramatic testimony, pushed him forward too fast. He suffered a public relapse. As far as I know no one offered him deliverance to sever the past generational sin, curses, and demonic attachments which would have been legally compelled as an evil assignment to hold on with a firm grip. I didn't offer this myself, although I might have. Needing, but not having received deliverance myself I was ignorant of how God might have used me. I'm convinced that some fall away from the faith because supernatural deliverance through which healing comes and then needed aftercare in whatever form that may be called for, is not offered.

I spent several days taping interviews with this man because I thought I'd like to write his family story. I was intrigued at the legacy of criminal behavior that seemed to have impacted all but one sibling. During that time I asked him if his Pastor and church ever offered Christian counseling to heal from the wounds of a traumatic and assaultive childhood. I was also interested to know if he had gained any insight about his mother who evidenced many evil traits in the ways that she groomed her children to care-take her physical and emotional needs even into adulthood, but about whom he had no apparent insight and showed blind loyalty.

An unhealthy soul tie keeps the narcissistic supply, a weaker person, readily available to the perpetrator. More about this later.

It is foolish to think that God doesn't call us to walk beside those that are saved... assisting as they work out their faith "in fear and trembling." Many fall away because the façade of a traditional and legalistic, or feelings based religious construct, fails to offer inner healing through counseling and deliverance. We are all sealed to eternal life at the moment of salvation, but we are not perfected as we will be when finally in heaven we exchange the corrupted body for new bodies. Spiritual growth is a process, a decision, a commitment. To this end God called the church as His body to love one another through accountability and healing. (*Ephesians 4: 20-24*)

Someone else I know has a son who is an addict whom she has faithfully prayed for over many years. I discerned that there was a generational curse giving satan legal access to this boy. When I introduced what I felt God had told me she politely listened, but clearly wasn't interested. A few weeks prior it was clear that the Lord had been speaking to her. She followed me to the parking lot and broached this topic which was why I had been seeking the Lord about this in the first place. Prompted by the pastor's sermon she emotionally asserted that she didn't believe, "that stuff about generational cures." The tragedy of this is that, as a believing parent, without her sons' cooperation, she has the authority to stand in for deliverance and break these strongholds. She can't control his choices, but she can assist the battle so that the preponderance of supernatural strength is for her son and not the enemy.

It is no coincidence that the following verse comes after a powerful and oft used Bible passage implemented as a significant weapon in deliverance and exorcism... words which memorized and believed upon, satan particularly hates. Read and memorize Philippians 2: 5-11. Continuing on, the next part reads... *So, then, my beloved, just as you have always obeyed, not as in my presence only, but now much more in my absence, work out your salvation with fear and trembling; for it is God who is at work in you, both to will and to work for His good pleasure (Philippians 2: 12, 13).*

We are sold a bill of goods if we don't realize that some new Christians need an ongoing deliverance in order to fully heal. Even before healing, curses need to be broken. Some believers have a powerful shepherding and teaching gift rooted in mercy. Those who have suffered need these relationships.

In their unsaved status the Willingly Influenced have a profane hatred of all that is Christ honoring. They regularly profane the name of Jesus Christ and have trouble appropriately containing such word curses. For others, hatred of the cross and Jesus Christ may be strategically disguised.

19

In a complicated process that is different for each person, the Willingly Influenced has allowed intelligent and personal evil to infiltrate their thinking. ***And just as they did not see fit to acknowledge God any longer, God gave them over to a depraved mind... (Romans 1: 28).*** As these lost souls become more committed to evil and bad behavior they begin to sense a preternatural component to their interior life that they sometimes describe in religious or occult terms and conversely conceal or flaunt in the exercise of religious or occult beliefs and practices.

The man I wrote of who came to Christ while in prison described many ritualistic practices that the family acted out, believing these rituals kept them safe from detection by law enforcement and in their dealings with other criminals. Although the name of satan was not specifically invoked, the power called upon was satanic. Each time these rituals, some quite detailed and disturbing, were exercised, demonic power was given legal authority to harness the behavior of those that willingly partnered and aligned themselves with darkness and in the end, the price paid was harsh indeed.

Many will never move beyond this state. Death bed confessions of faith occur with the willingly influenced as I describe in the second book in the Wood's End series, *The Year Between the Wood,* with the fictional character of Herb.

In deliverance we find that these people have a demonic stronghold from which they need freedom. Many are physically ill with diseases which have set up in their bodies as evidence of certain infestations. We feel compassion and want to see these people free to embrace the love and healing that is Jesus Christ, our Savior.

Believers engaged in healing ministries confront these amalgams of practice which have at the root, demonic infestation. In facing a serious physical illness some may show up at healing services brought by friends who assume they are Christians.

I feel strongly that there needs to be some interaction and preparation, asking if people presenting for healing prayer do, in fact, have a personal relationship with Jesus Christ. I interviewed Pastor Mike Frisbee on my internet radio show. He described phoning a prayer line because he was facing surgery and in horrible pain. At the time Mike was heavily into witchcraft and was the head of a satanic coven. The person on the other end of the phone exercised her gift of discerning spirits. She suggested he first confess his sins and pray for salvation in Jesus Christ. In this way Mike was led to the Lord by a woman who acted on what God revealed; discerning with spiritual sight what wasn't said in words. Jesus Christ physically healed Mike so that the scheduled surgery was not needed.

Healing and deliverance ministries are so tied together that in Jesus' example and teaching we see the connections very clearly demonstrated throughout the gospels. *At that very time He cured many people of diseases and afflictions and evil spirits (Luke 7: 21a).*

We cannot but help recognize the scriptural connections between disease, affliction, and evil spirits and ultimately a powerful supernatural encounter with the Savior, Jesus Christ as the one eternal answer.

While the sun was setting, all those who had any who were sick with various diseases brought them to Him; and laying His hands on each one of them, He was healing them. Demons also were coming out of many, shouting, "You are the Son of God!" But rebuking them, He would not allow them to speak, because they knew Him to be the Christ (Luke 4: 40, 41).

I love that God instructs us to pray in His name, requiring that demons and evil spirits remain silent. There are many reasons why we follow Christ's example in this. That, however, would be a book for another time.

CHAPTER THREE

THREE CLASSES OF POSSESSION: DIFFERENT SYMPTOMS – ONE SOLUTION

Now, with broad brush, we'll look at three states of demon possession. Although we might logically view these three states as a progression, the one leading to the next this is not always the case. All these people need the Savior, Jesus Christ. They need deliverance through exorcism. They are not Christians.

Others who may need deliverance are Christians that experience little victory in their lives, read and remember little scripture, exhibit self-defeating behavior, and have a generational history of besetting sins as patterns of practice. They may have, in the generational history, an ambulatory or fatally possessed direct-bloodline ancestor, even four or so generations back. They may also have peripherally suffered under the life stealing control of a narcissistic parent, caretaker, perpetrator, or elder sibling in which case they have unhealed trauma upon which defeat camps.

I've termed the three states of possession as follows.
- The Conflicted Possessed
- The Ambulatory Possessed
- The Fatally Possessed

The Conflicted Possessed, have consciously invited a demon/demons to inhabit their bodies. Self-will has broken down. That marvelous gift given to all human beings, the ability to self-determine a course of action, has been severely disabled and then subverted. A gauge of health is that healthy people know when they are "sick" and can ask for what they need. These people are in danger of forever losing this God given ability.

If they remember what happened and can later report, they will describe moving from a place of feeling conflicted over abdicating control to a seducing spirit, to finally giving in. When this happens, some part of them is instantly, completely, and utterly repelled by what they have invited to cohabit their flesh. By God-given instinct, but too late the fatal danger is recognized. From deep within, where human willpower transcends material space, they put up a valiant fight to restore the lost autonomy. They feel this loss as a profound shock to core sensibilities. The promised power, peace, place, or benefits do not materialize as anticipated and unimaginable suffering takes place. They are desperate for a do-over. They long to go back in time and shout a resounding, "NO!"

The manifestations of possession are revealed to others in a visible battle for complete and total possession of the host body. The object is not always physical death. This is because demons have lost their home in heaven and seek significance through a host body. In Luke, chapter eight, the demons, once cast out of the body, begged to enter the swine.

This victim, who evidences such extreme behavior, is often mistakenly thought to be in worse shape than the person who is ambulatory possessed and operational. Not true. In the conflicted possessed these tragic people are "conflicted" about what has happened. They are not accepting, and are still fighting in defense of their souls. For this reason, those conducting the exorcism have a cooperating soul beneath all the horror that manifests. As the demons are silenced and human spirits are bound back to their bodies, the exorcist can guide this person to the throne of grace. The Conflicted Possessed are more likely to be freed, restored and healed than those in the ambulatory class of demonic possession and manifestation.

Conflicted Possession is the picture most often depicted in movies like *The Exorcist*. In this, and similar films, the victim will evidence some symptoms in common with severe psychosis. ***They were so extremely violent that no one could pass by that way (Matthew 8: 28b); ...and no one was able to bind him anymore, even with a chain (Mark 5: 3b). Constantly, night and day, he was screaming among the tombs and in the mountains, and gashing himself with stones (Mark 5: 5).***

There are significant and telling differences between the mentally ill and the Conflicted Possessed. Read **Mark 5: 1-20, Luke 8: 26-39**, and **Matthew 8: 28-34**. There is usually no history of mental illness. This person will display super-human strength and is outwardly violent and self mutilating, has information common persons are not privy to, and can emit an indescribable foul scent that waxes and wanes, but isn't always smelled by all persons at the same time. They speak in tones outside a normal human voice and do sometimes speak in other languages; even dead languages. In all forms of possession there are times when the skin appears stretched across the face with facial contortions which, though fleeting, are also offensive; even shocking.

The Ambulatory Possessed are operational in the world. It is sometimes a first challenge of the leader associated with the deliverance team to make sure this person is, in fact Ambulatory Possessed. We can confuse what presents as Willingly Influenced which changes how we approach and plan for a godly outcome.

The Willingly Influenced will have demons and will need deliverance and inner healing in aftercare as they walk out a new freedom, free to love and serve Jesus Christ. They come by choice, having recognized the need and seeking intervention. The Willingly Influenced will not present the level of resistance that an Ambulatory Possessed person presents. The Ambulatory Possessed will very rarely and almost never legitimately seek freedom, because the self and self-will has been given over to demonic control to a far greater degree. It is often a family member or even a Christian counselor who initiates the exorcism. If they do seek help of their own volition, a miracle has occurred as a precursor to a successful exorcism. What follows, is ongoing deliverance and inner healing, God's divine plan and process for a new and fully functional restoration.

The primary demon, not willing to give up the host body, may seem to cooperate so as to deceive the team and prematurely end the effort. Freedom and exorcism in this context requires an experienced and anointed leader. The end goal is to make sure this person understands what has happened and is ready to receive Jesus Christ as Savior. If not we haven't helped them. *...and the last state of that man becomes worse than the first.* Excerpt from *Matthew 12: 43-45*.

Christian intercessors/prayer warriors are called to be involved and to support a healing and deliverance ministry, but fewer saints wear the actual mantle and authority of an on-site, hands-on Exorcist. Satan is the consummate legalist. For this reason, an Exorcist is one called and anointed; appointed before they were born and sometimes life-trained even before they are scripturally informed and sealed to eternal salvation. Bill Bean, Father Malachi Martin, Judith MacNutt, Ken Thornberg, and Mayaba Choongo are a few examples of such a destiny. The Exorcist knows who he/she is and they have an awareness of being recognized by angels and demons. God has given them a companion gift of healing which always imbues a strong faith. They discern spirits and have spiritual sight. They are not denominationally authorized, but Holy Spirit compelled. They would be an Exorcist whether catholic or protestant and they may be male or female, but more often male.

In order to become Ambulatory Possessed there must first be a void. There may be a genetic flaw, a head trauma or past brain surgery that fundamentally alters the physical guarding and checking mechanisms that God originally intended all persons to have. This person may have been born into a satanic cult, or a dangerous household, or a pagan culture where systematic and sophisticated mind control coupled with physical abuse is perpetrated on children. Though the etiology is diverse and disguised, there has been a greater and greater seeking after the occult and occult powers. What follows is a commitment to evil behavior which fundamentally changes the brain so that a person is callous and unfeeling, allowing demons to enter and seek a territorial stronghold from which to wage war.

There may be transformations brought about by certain chemical addictions. The addictive lifestyle is in itself evil and opens the door to progressing levels of demonic infestation and growing partnership with evil spirits. Being part of new age and occult systems and false religions facilitates one becoming Ambulatory Possessed. *But the Spirit explicitly says that in later times some will fall away from the faith, paying attention to deceitful spirits and doctrines of demons, by means of the hypocrisy of liars seared in their own conscience as with a branding iron (1st Timothy 4: 1, 2).*

The psychology of who gets possessed by evil and who doesn't is not fathomable. There is no logic connecting the dots that allow us to trace the same path for each person. There are commonalities and striking patterns that set up via crucial decisions, but not for all persons. Some just have a scripted path and no conscience or ability to feel empathy. No attempt at psycho-babble can fully explain this. God created us as individuals. So there are no easy explanations or infallible sequence of cause and effect. Much of what we'll learn about possession has to be viewed next to that of psychopaths and a firm belief that evil is personal and exists beyond the human body as a condemned source of hatred. Science and spiritual truths of God will reveal much of what we need to know, but for all intents and purposes this needed partnership, with God and faith taking preeminence, will be resisted as it always has been.

Evil has traditionally been a religious word and using this word, even in the church, has been seen as harsh. Christian writers have introduced broader, even clinical concepts of what is evil. We are wise to tread carefully when dealing with the Ambulatory Possessed who, appear on the outside to be perfectly normal, even charismatically charming, but are in fact dangerous.

I recommend, as valuable reading, Dr. Michael H. Stone's scale of evil; *The Anatomy of Evil (Prometheus Books; 2009; ISBN-13: 978-1-59102-726-3)*. His work gives an excellent context to our consideration of these people as we apply Biblical constructs to some of the emerging psycho and bio-medical knowledge. As you confront a situation and make a determination as a believer, it's helpful to have an understanding of Dr. Stone's important research. Again, while the Ambulatory Possessed, are candidates for exorcism, they will almost never present for help. They are prevented by the demonic infestation to which their human will is subjugated in a satanic death-grip of wretched toxicity.

We do, however, meet the victims of the Ambulatory Possessed and here is where the deliverance and healing calling gets applied to glorious outcomes. These sufferers are in desperate need of deliverance. Their courage to disclose directs our response and may even, bring perpetrators to justice. Stripping away the truth in order to help someone self protect against those relationships that are not easily severed is an important role played by a deliverance ministry in aftercare and counseling.

An example of one who was Ambulatory Possessed is Judas. *The chief priests and the scribes were seeking how they might put Him to death; for they were afraid of the people. And Satan entered into Judas who was called Iscariot, belonging to the number of the twelve (Luke 22: 2, 3). After the morsel, Satan then entered into him. Therefore Jesus said to him, "What you do, do quickly" (John 13: 27).*

So here we see that evil needs a human conduit (Judas) and that Jesus Christ, for a holy purpose, allowed the preternatural partnership between Judas and the Hebrew religious authority to unfold. Hopefully we do not miss the fact that a literal satan, as a fallen spirit-being, literally entered into Judas, who then became Ambulatory Possessed.

Not in the least evidencing any psychosis, the battle lost on some profound level, the newly possessed Judas very effectively enters into negotiations for the betrayal of Jesus. At no time do we read that Judas displays the kind of internal fight of a masking psychosis as seen in the demoniac from the tombs who was Conflicted Possessed. What we have is a different sub-class or form of possession which tells us something about how we formulate a Christian response.

Jesus did not, after the fact, orchestrate the kind of exorcism for Judas that He provided to the demoniac from the tombs. *"At the name of Jesus every knee shall bow."* Read in full: *Philippians 10: 5-11. The people went out to see what had happened; and they came to Jesus, and found the man from whom the demons had gone out, sitting down at the feet of Jesus, clothed and in his right mind... (Luke 8: 35a).*

Later we read that Judas was tormented to suicide by the possessing horde, which lets us know that he was not fatally possessed. Fatally possessed people do not evidence any glimmer of remorse and would not feel depressed which implies regret. People who are Ambulatory Possessed are satanically tasked, as Judas was, to operate outside the sphere of recognition for as long as possible or until God decides, enough is enough. Often the catalyst of recognition comes through the actions and prayers of former victims, now engaged in a deliverance ministry.

The Ambulatory Possessed can be successfully freed to the glory of Jesus Christ, but it is rare that they ask for help. When they do we should examine how manipulative that request may be as a measure to avoid some kind of pending consequence. On the other hand we know that Paul, who was a murderer and fanatic hater of "this new way" when he stepped from ***"darkness to light, from the dominion of Satan to God"*** was instantly healed of the possessing demonic partnerships that had driven him to act in cooperation with a satanic strategy.

If Conflicted Possessed victims move into being Ambulatory Possessed they are no longer fighting their previous battle in the same way. This is reflected in how the demons operate within the flesh of that person who has given up the fight and abandoned a certain level of intense resistance. They now become operational and enter the world as the enemy of those around them. If previously restrained in a hospital bed, they can now present as "cured." The façade may at times break away and they will display signs of remorse, attempt suicide, or abuse themselves in attention getting ways. This should be discerned as different from the primary demon handler allowing the body to attempt suicide in order to mitigate legal consequences which may cut off operational access to future victims.

The Ambulatory Possessed, including white collar criminals have an uncanny history of skating on legal charges. Satanic pedophile perpetrators are too often aided by satanic partnerships in the legal arena. An example is Yellowstone County district judge, G. Todd Baugh who sentenced Montana teacher Stacey Rambold to 30 days in jail for the rape of a fourteen year old girl who later committed suicide.

Deflecting attention from this decision, and making a travesty of the excellent work of prosecutors, Judge Baugh blamed the victim. I have no proof, but I believe that Ray Gricar, officially, but not in practice, ever closed the Sandusky pedophile case. Enlisting the help of his brother, who also died, he had awareness of a far larger criminal conspiracy making the decision to take his investigation under-ground.

Sex abuse is another form of ritualistically sacrificing children to satan. The Department of Children's Services in Tennessee could not even accurately say how many children died in their care in 2012. They redacted crucial information from records and refused disclosure to the media until a judge overruled their attempts to avoid accountability. When will we begin to recognize the abuse of and failure to protect children, as an organized satanic agenda under the direction of territorial evil spirits grooming and making use of human beings as passive facilitators and perpetrators? The imprint, the infestation, the influence...

Such a history of escaping legal consequences can be part of the body of evidence that finally contributes to recognition of evil people and satanic agendas. Many of God's children called to work in law enforcement might consciously pray for the discernment and courage to act on suspicions which others ignore. Develop the skill of exercising the spiritual gift of discerning spirits. Know and embrace these intuitive inclinations and demand that proof deserves appropriate investigation.

As psychopaths, the Ambulatory Possessed manifest extreme behavioral perversions. They may be active in a satanic group or attending a fringe-pseudo or salt-less "Christian" church. Ritualistic child abuse and serial murder become a frightening manifestation. Others follow their greed compulsions and are addicted con-artists. Suicide of victims is a byproduct of white collar criminals like Bernie Madoff. Writer, radio talk show host, and investigative journalist Rick Baker says that we will never know how many people committed suicide over fraudulent loss of homes and savings associated with the actions of corrupt banking institutions and the greed of contractors and foreclosure sub-servicers that continue to feed on victims caught in the housing turmoil.

The Ambulatory Possessed will go to great lengths to shroud their activities in secrecy. An example from film is *Mr. Brooks*. At the start of the film Earl Brooks is receiving a community service award. This main character in the film is a serial killer and is also Ambulatory Possessed. We see a primary demon handler, but there would be untold numbers of other demons present and working through his body. The primary demon handler, played so well by William Hurt, is threatened when Earl attends Alcoholics Anonymous meetings in a futile attempt to contain the homicidal compulsions that are decimating his humanity. Clever writing in the metaphor of him manufacturing boxes, because the once person is in a box and is the box that might as well be a coffin.

Some are in our midst as agents of satan, under satanic assignment to operate in the church. An example is a high profile church I'm aware of that for decades harbored a pedophile on staff in a position of authority. One of the victims grew up and became

29

healthy enough to confront the system that failed to protect him and other children when they were most vulnerable. When this information threatened to "go public" a cadre of church members, were more concerned with the legacy of the recently deceased Senior Pastor than with reporting and then offering help to victims.

Some are in positions of authority on the world stage to thwart God's plan and purpose for the universe, and yet God has historically restrained satan's purpose for these human-evil conduits, not allowing them the unbridled access they would like. Preternatural information is exchanged and these people are, at some point, unmasked by the possessing demons that realize the authorities are closing in. God may have them compulsively act out the death agenda in ways that get them caught. This can be seen in the last reckless killing spree of Ted Bundy. Additionally, in the final assaults of serial killer Glen Rogers whose brother, Clay Rogers, revealed startling insight. Clay said in an interview, "I wasn't turning in my brother. I was turning in a serial killer. My brother hadn't lived there in a long time." Clay also expressed an understanding that his brother's primary demon, the body itself an empty conduit, was tasked with passing on the demonic infestation to him.

Recognizing and restraining evil is the responsibility of Christian people, difficult to accomplish when the religious church can hardly utter the word "evil" for fear of offending or being politically incorrect. An important role of believers is to protect those who are at risk of proximity to demonically controlled individuals or systems. Well meaning persons can be drawn into the field of demonic influence and become passive facilitators, numb to outrage and in danger of the same fate. It can be discerned at some point that the demonized person no longer can separate their own person-hood and thoughts from the possessing infestation. Over time there are fewer and fewer glimpses of the once living persona.

Christians in law enforcement who commit to a full understanding can be powerfully used by God for justice. Their work and investigative skills, deductive reasoning and godly instinct are only enhanced by an understanding of how demons operate through human vessels. Learning to pray against the imprint, the infestation, and the influence God imparts supernatural insight and direction. One specific prayer could be that communication in the unseen world of evil is confused so that perpetrators are apprehended sooner rather than later. Jesus loves justice and gives special grace to those that partner in exposing evil.

Sex does not usually happen with the Conflicted Possessed because they evidence such levels of violence and psychiatric disturbance. The Ambulatory Possessed are either asexual or they engage in sex as a ritual of dominance and violence; an enmeshing kind of rite which reflects the evil mandate to virulently assault all life. Many are pedophiles and rapists. Victims or partners may report seeing the demonic face revealed in the act of sex which becomes the impetus to separate from such a relationship.

A life cut short by murder or toxic enmeshment is potentially a life that will never live in the light of Christ and becomes by proxy a territorial possession of satan, part of the company consigned to hell.

The Fatally Possessed, are people who have no shred left within of anything that remotely resembles God's human creation. There is but one unpardonable sin that closes the door to salvation and only the Fatally Possessed, have committed this sin.

If you worry that you have committed the unpardonable sin – you have not. The Fatally Possessed have, lost the God-given capacity for self examination. They receive no censure and no longer experience conviction. Walking and talking, lethal and charming, they embody the spirit of satan, masquerading as an angel of light only to reveal the ravenous lion seeking whom it can destroy.

To think we can reason or appease these people, is to invite a ravenous lion to tea. Our job is to recognize them and then formulate a plan to destroy them. In the movie, *Tea with Mussolini,* based on a true story, the Maggie Smith character believes she has a special reciprocal connection with Mussolini. As World War 11 wages on, her loyalties are divided since she is an English woman trapped behind enemy lines in fascist Italy. She and Mussolini did actually have tea together... once. While in captivity, she drags their pathetic photo commemorating this event around with her. The truth is, she spoke a human language to which he, as a Fatally Possessed vehicle was deaf and blind. Only when her delusions are dismantled by a confrontation with honesty does she face her error.

These are the real monsters of childhood nightmares that function fairly efficiently as the embodiment of evil. The antichrist of Revelation will be Fatally Possessed. When the Fatally Possessed, cross paths with us, as discerning believers, we should know that we are in the presence of something alien. Having this awareness means that we have trained our senses to know the difference between good and evil, being receptive to what the Holy Spirit supernaturally conveys, long before evidence reveals the truth.

There is no hope for the Fatally Possessed. The Christian role is to expose and end the reign of terror. The Fatally Possessed are reflected in the strongholds they occupy; the illegal drug industry, sex for sale, or any societal or pseudo cult arena where they can impact trend and undermine all that is decent and good in the exercise of personal and intentional evil.

Some governments are a reflection of a systemic necrosis and the evil they perpetrate on their people, and the wars they engage in are satanic agendas. Others hold sway over very small areas which we would almost not recognize, but for the powerful and significant imprint of evil and the iron on iron Holy Spirit discernment acuity at work through us. Take heed of and utilize your instincts. Practice your God-given supernatural skills of discernment. Pray and ask God to reveal the truth. Let God lead you into further investigation and in this, partner with other believing Christians.

Through the ages satan has thrust many of the fatally possessed onto the world stage in an effort to control and manipulate God's predetermined time table for future events. Such futile efforts will always fail. Satan has already been judged.

CHAPTER FOUR

READY FOR SERVICE

...for you have been born again not of seed which is perishable but imperishable, that is, through the living and enduring word of God (1st Peter 1: 23).

All those drawn by the Holy Spirit to the practice of deliverance and exorcism need to get three very common human obstacles behind them.

1. **LOOKING HOMEWARD** – Where do you live? As new born babies, at the very start of this temporal existence we opened our eyes on the arena of warfare. The Son of God, Jesus Christ willingly offered Himself as the Savior of all who would call on His name when he entered planet earth via a human mother; the virgin Mary. *And the dragon stood before the woman who was about to give birth, so that when she gave birth he might devour her child (Revelation 12: 4b).* We are God's children and the church is His body. God's sacrifice on the cross, His love for us, has drawn and anchored us to Christ. Deliverance from evil spirits, from evil people commandeered as instruments of opposition, and healing from physical illness was and is a daily and consistent outcome of the battle waged well.

We began life completely dependent. If those charged with our care did not love, if we began life in a region of the globe at war or during a period of human history wracked by turmoil we were in trouble. Then there were the childhood diseases to overcome. There were also the inherited curses and blessings. *Deuteronomy 28: 15-46* describe the curses; *Deuteronomy 28: 1-14* describe the blessings. We fought this battle for ongoing life and sustenance and behind the scenes, in dimensions we couldn't see other battles were waged over the territories of body, will, and soul.

The miracle of God in our lives guides, rescues, and nourishes. *Blessed be the Lord, who daily bears our burden, the God who is our salvation. God is to us a God of deliverances; and to God the Lord belong escapes from death (Psalm 68: 19, 20).*

The majority of these escapes occur without us ever being aware. The Holy Spirit lives within, while ministering and warring angels have our back. *For He will give His angels charge concerning you, to guard you in all your ways. They will bear you up in their hands, that you do not strike your foot against a stone (Psalms 91: 11, 12).*

Where do you live? Does some part of you long for home, an internal song rising up from the deep well of your emotional life, the eternal stamp of a heavenly existence, though dimly felt and yet, a very real yearning? *For now we see in a mirror dimly, but then face to face; now I know in part, but then I will know fully just as I also have been fully known (1ˢᵗ Corinthians 13: 12).*

With your feet on earth and your loyalty fixed in the realm of faith, how do you maneuver the conundrums related to this question? Not merely in the temporal plane of planet earth, but in your mind and in the stuff and flow of daily life, in routine and crisis, in conflicts and celebrations, in loss and disappointment, in gain and favor. Calling yourself a Christian the answer determines how well you'll live for Christ, whether you'll frame your choices and responses with eternity in mind. The Apostle Paul made clear where his loyalties and sensibilities fell on this question. *For I consider that the sufferings of this present time are not worthy to be compared with the glory that is to be revealed to us (Romans 8: 18).*

What risks you'll take for Him, what sacrifices you'll make or not make in defense of character, and bottom line... how effectively you will grasp and wield your God-given status and tools of warfare is up to you. Stepping into the realm of faith these weapons are powerful indeed. If they are rusty and little used it is never too late to take them off the shelf, to clean and prime, to load and arm *...for the weapons of our warfare are not of the flesh, but divinely powerful for the destruction of fortresses (2ⁿᵈ Corinthians 10: 4).*

You are a prince or princess in the royal family of the Most High God. You are temporarily assigned to planet Earth. *So then you are no longer strangers and aliens, but you are fellow citizens with the saints and are of God's household, having been built on the foundation of the apostles and prophets, Christ Jesus Himself being the corner stone... (Ephesians 2: 19, 20).*

Where do you live? Looking homeward, it will be your joy and privilege to fight well.

2. **WHOSE APPROVAL ARE WE AFTER?** Once we've decided to live for Christ on His terms and according to His word there is a profound, mysterious, and exciting shift that takes place.

This is a far grander and more wondrous life that plumbs the depths of faith to which all believers are called to aspire and then play an important role. Why, you may ask... *so that the manifold wisdom of God might now be made known through the church to the rulers and the authorities in the heavenly places (Ephesians 3: 10).*

A fundamental change in perception and allegiance blossoms and deepens. *For our citizenship is in heaven, from which also we eagerly wait for a Savior, the Lord Jesus Christ, who will transform the body of our humble state into conformity with the body of His glory, by the exertion of the power that He has even to subject all things to Himself (Philippians 3: 20, 21).*

This shift was clearly manifested and expressed in scripture. Paul asked this rhetorical question: *For am I now seeking the favor of men, or of God? Or am I striving to please men?* Paul then answers the question. *If I were still trying to please men, I would not be a bond servant of Christ (Galatians 1:10).*

There is always a cause and effect outcome to any change. By definition change requires a shift that moves an area of passivity to action or abruptly shifts a moving trajectory onto an altered course or path. Pleasing God and walking to the divine mandate is our highest priority. Though separated in most Bibles by a subheading that shouldn't be there the passage continues. *For I would have you know, brethren, that the gospel which was preached by me is not according to man. For I neither received it from man, nor was I taught it, but I received it through a revelation of Jesus Christ (Galatians 1: 12).*

Through experience and trial God equips and molds us. I love the intimate analogy of the next verse. Though there were times when we didn't see it, His hand was ever upon us, His beloved sons and daughters. *But now, O Lord, You are our Father, we are the clay, and You our potter; and all of us are the work of Your hand (Isaiah 64: 8).*

There are unseen realms which co-exist those that are seen. Prayer literally enters these dimensions and unleashes Godly force and angelic armies. Transported via prayer into the arena of deliverance, we bind the opposition, partnering with God in doing what is His divine nature to do – restore, heal, and free from bondage.

A truly beautiful picture of what transpires in deliverance prayer, in any heartfelt prayer, is the "where" and "with whom" we actually stand, transported by Holy Spirit conveyance into the unseen realm in order to impact destiny. In shedding the constraint of pleasing men we are no longer bound by religious traditions and fear of what others think. As we leave the material constraints behind, we experience the awe of being in God's presence.

But you have come to Mount Zion and to the city of the living God, the heavenly Jerusalem, and to myriads of angels, to the general assembly and the church of the first born who are enrolled in heaven, and to God, the Judge of all, and to the spirits of the righteous made perfect, and to Jesus, the mediator of a new covenant, and to the sprinkled blood, which speaks better than the blood of Abel (Hebrews 12: 22-24).

So embroiled with externals we may forget to consider the inward substance of the lies we've adopted. Nor do we examine the philosophical constructs or the intellectual and emotional triggers common within the societal framework from which the enemy seeks to program our responses. Even as some strive for self-control there is little victory. It is from all this and more that the human creation, over which cosmic battles wage, that personal deliverance is needed. *But if I cast out demons by the Spirit of God, then the kingdom of God has come upon you. Or how can anyone enter the strongman's house and carry off his property, unless he first binds the strong man? And then he will plunder his house (Matthew 12: 28, 29).*

3. **APOSTASY** is the third obstacle to overcome. We must guard against religious structures that reconfigure and deliberately misinterpret or rewrite the word of God in order to attract funds and people. Traditions, feel good scripts, and worship as entertainment is no substitute for Christ's power.

Religion is not, nor has it ever been, the radical transforming faith of true Christianity. Many denominational faiths that began as powerful movements of evangelism are now neutered in apostasy. Every denomination has needed correction. All have gone through cycles which mirror the falling away and then the penitent denouncement of corruption, sin, and institutional scandal associated with turns toward paganism. There are many struggling Christian priests and pastors enslaved by denominational fear. Too many of these, called of the Lord, give up the fight and leave service. In Christian, Biblical faith we can only have God on His terms – a genuine, interactive reverence for and intimate fellowship with the Lamb of God, Jesus Christ. *...that if you confess with your mouth Jesus as Lord, and believe in your heart that God raised Him from the dead you shall be saved; for with the heart a person believes, resulting in righteousness, and with the mouth he confesses, resulting in salvation*

(Romans 10: 9, 10).

In Second Kings 22 and 23 we read of a time when the Book of the Law was lost to the people. In the same way today some of God's teachings have been so marginalized as to be lost. Where responsibility is given over a void exists. Every void represents an open invitation for demonic infestations to set up shop as a snare for human-kind. Behind every idol and travesty of faith are these strongholds from which demons operate, empowered by the three core motivations for all sin; greed, lust, power. ***Therefore there will be a visitation also upon the heathen idols, because, though part of what God created, they became an abomination, snares for human souls and a trap for the feet of the foolish (The Wisdom of Solomon 14: 11).***

When we read ***2ⁿᵈ Kings, chapters 22, 23*** we see that the people no longer had room for, nor remembered, **Father God**, the great **I AM** who, in a visible demonstration of love and mercy -- for a divine purpose delivered their ancestors and all subsequent generations out of slavery in Egypt. This sin of forgetfulness had meant a tragic societal, cultural and religious plunge into the practice of sorceries and enchantments. Detestable items used in worship to demons had been allowed into the temple defiling a place that had once been set aside to the holiness of God.

One day a lost and forgotten book was discovered in the temple. ***Then Hilkiah the high priest said to Shaphan the scribe, "I have found the book of the law in the house of the Lord" (2ⁿᵈ Kings 22: 8).***

What followed this momentous discovery was massive reform. All the Hebrew high holy days were reinstituted, including Passover. Then revival arrived in a supernatural visitation of God at work through individuals to effect dramatic, visible, lasting and radical change via true repentance. From that time forward King Josiah stayed the course; ***nor did he turn aside to the right or to the left (2ⁿᵈ Kings 22: 2b).*** For his faithfulness and willingness to confront apostasy the young King Josiah has never been forgotten. ***Surely such a Passover had not been celebrated from the days of the judges who judged Israel, nor in all the days of the kings of Israel and of the Kings of Judah (2ⁿᵈ Kings 23: 22).***

Apostasy within the traditional church is among the signs which precede judgment. Among the forgotten teachings in far too many pulpits are the teachings and warning against the occult. Anyone called to the practice of healing and deliverance may need to unlearn what most religious organizations teach; if in fact they attend a church that even takes a position on these topics.

Just as the Book of Law, The Torah, was rediscovered and pulled from the upheaval of renovation many of us, as true believers, need a renovation of heart and mind. We must re-discover the Bible; reading it for ourselves and using several accepted translations. *For the word of God is living and active and sharper than any two-edged sword, and piercing as far as the division of soul and spirit, of both joints and marrow, and able to judge the thoughts and intentions of the heart. And there is no creature hidden from His sight... (Hebrews 4: 12, 13a).*

That a Christian has trouble reading scripture and praying is clear evidence that they need inner healing and deliverance.

BACK TO BASICS

Therefore I urge you brethren, by the mercies of God, to present your bodies a living and holy sacrifice, acceptable to God, which is your spiritual service of worship. And do not be conformed to this world, but be transformed by the renewing of your mind, so that you may prove what is good and acceptable and perfect (Romans 12: 1, 2).

True bond servants of Christ are not conformists. God cannot use us effectively in the unseen realm to impact the destiny of our loved ones, if we are still trying to please men. For some this means being in bondage to misapplications of scripture which are conforming to denominational influences and societal indoctrination and not to the fullness of faith in Jesus Christ. Pray and ask right now that God will open your eyes to any part you have played in furthering a "different gospel." *I am amazed that you are so quickly deserting Him who called you by the grace of Christ, for a different gospel... (Galatians 1: 6).*

And where does Paul say this threat comes from? *As we have said before, so I say again now, if any man is preaching to you a gospel contrary to what you received, he is to be accursed! (Galatians 1: 9).* Sad to say, in this current period of world history the threat comes primarily from the religious church.

As you continue to stand in the area of deliverance, using the tools described in scripture, the battle changes as you grow. You are regularly dispatching demons to the throne of God for immediate judgment, asking that they be sent to the abyss never to return and asking that God would burn with the fire of the Holy Spirit any backups or replacements; sending them to the abyss as well, never to return. Satan will soon realize that the losses associated with your personal walk of faith are great. You'll always be tested, but you'll also be called to greater levels of interactive clashes which grows the awe we feel for Christ; wanting to know

Him better and feeling a joy and anointing that transcends any oppositional circumstance; seen or unseen.

BATTLE READINESS

If we can accept our status as alien residents on planet earth, if we can shed the bondage of conformity, if we can read God's word and believe what it says, we act as the righteousness of God in Christ to impact the destiny of this world and those we love. Once the area of deliverance is opened up to us, the experiences God allows will further grow and change us.

Though the Lord may give you the bread of adversity and the water of affliction, yet your Teacher will not hide himself anymore (Isaiah 30: 20). In a tangible way never experienced before we have looked into the face of evil, and evil has glared back. We have marked the presence of angels and perhaps even seen them. The Holy Spirit has prophetically revealed information and in this we've been further equipped by the ever-present voice of God directing our steps. *And when you turn to the right or when you turn to the left, your ears shall hear a word behind you, saying, "This is the way; walk in it" (Isaiah 30: 21).*

In seeing what can't be easily explained in a material construct the eyes of our heart open. Faith grows as awareness shifts and we realize something profound. We truly are the church-militant and armed with the love God extended to us as a supernatural, indwelling presence we must share that love. In that desire we cherish God's living Holy Spirit and do nothing to impede Jesus working in and through us. It is for battle that we prefer obedience. It is for battle that He has equipped us in the love that passes all understanding and shatters all satanic barriers. Scripture says what it means and means what it says. *He is clothed with a robe dipped in blood, and His name is called The Word of God (Revelation 19: 13). ...so that at the name of Jesus every knee will bow, of those who are in heaven and on earth and under the earth, and that every tongue will confess that Jesus Christ is Lord, to the glory of God the Father (Philippians 2: 10, 11).*

YOUR CALLING is powerful indeed. In *Galatians chapter 1*, the apostle Paul lays it out, stating his position in Christ. *Paul, an apostle (not sent from men nor through the agency of man, but through Jesus Christ and God the Father, who raised Him from the dead), and all the brethren who are with me. (Galatians 1: 1).*

The church does not commission you. A degree from a seminary does not authorize you. All believers have the Holy Spirit and therefore the ability to grow visionary capability. *But you are a chosen race, a royal priesthood, a holy nation, a people for God's own possession, so that you may proclaim the excellencies of Him who called you out of darkness into His marvelous light (1st Peter 2: 9). Ephesians 1: 17-23; Philippians 2: 5-11.* If you struggle with truly believing these words confess that as sin. Ask your Lord and Savior, Jesus Christ, to open the full mystery of understanding; renewing your mind and restoring your soul. We all perform different functions in the body of Christ and yet, God speaks to us about the calling that is uniquely ours. Asking Him for direction is like a child asking a parent if they can stop watching television and do homework.

All His promises to you are "yes" and "Amen." *For in Him every one of God's promises is a "Yes." For this reason it is through Him that we say the "Amen," to the glory of God (2nd Corinthians 1: 20).* Standing in the strength of your divine calling you will always have His promises. They are a divine right of inheritance. Ask God for the equipping that you need and then commit to that place where calling leads.

A really dangerous teaching of many denominations today is that there is no more revelation to be had and therefore the gift of prophecy is not relevant. This immediately cordons off whole areas of service and fixes power in the realm of the religious. This postures the false premise that visionary gifts should be removed from service in the body of Christ. Cults foster ignorance. True faith ever grows our anointing to hear from God. Visionary gifts have never left the body of Christ; yet, they are tragically marginalized and stifled per a satanic agenda. Some have the idea that we should all be the same which is the lie that distorts truth and neuters power. Sameness and conformity has never been evidence of godliness.

The church age is the last age prior to the return of Christ. This is the singular time and age that God deemed you and I would be born into and whose destiny we are charged to impact for His glory. The vital and important role, that visionary gifts play during our current age, was prophesized in the book of Joel; *Joel 33: 14-18.* This prophecy was repeated for further emphasis, commission, and clarity so that we would not miss the significance; *Acts 2: 17-21.* Read these verses together and in context. In part... *'And it shall be in the last days,' God says, 'That I will pour forth of My Spirit on all mankind; and your sons and your daughters shall prophesy, and your young men shall see visions, and your old men shall dream dreams (Acts 2: 17).*

It grieves me that so many labor under false denominational constraints, trained to dismiss the supernatural and denying themselves the power of a vibrant prayer life that is their right and calling to exercise. Simply put, revelation is you and I hearing from God. An acquaintance of mine lost her daughter in a tragic automobile accident. It was a bright beautiful morning when the car was struck by an oncoming motorist, blinded by the sun at a rural crossing. A woman stopped to help. As she covered the girl with her own coat, trying to stem off shock she spoke of Jesus and in the minutes before the last breath was taken prayed with the girl to affirm her faith in Jesus Christ.

After the funeral and at an appointed time, which the Holy Spirit revealed by revelation, this passer-by knocked on the family's door to share what she knew of the last minutes of this girls life. Not only was the mother grateful to know her daughter was not alone, scared and fatally bleeding, as she had imagined, but she also came to faith in Christ.

More often than not I will begin thinking one thing and the Holy Spirit will reveal something entirely different. I can choose to ignore the prompting of what I've understood or I can move forward and take this ever deeper. The minimal response would be to ask for confirmation. God trains us in this way to sharpen the eyes of our heart for what is happening in the unseen realm. If we stop to appraise what we hear and the answer is yes, we'd better act. "Father God, is what I'm discerning in this situation true? Is it false?"

But a natural man does not accept the things of the Spirit of God, for they are foolishness to him; and he cannot understand them, because they are spiritually appraised. But he who is spiritual appraises all things, yet he himself is appraised by no one. For who has known the mind of the Lord, that He will instruct Him. But we have the mind of Christ (1st Corinthians 2: 14-16).

We have *the mind of Christ.* Spiritual discernment manifests when we receive by faith what He is telling us. This allows us to see with the eyes of our heart and act in the confidence of faith as we walk in the *surpassing power of His greatness... And He put all things in subjection under His feet, and gave Him as head over all things to the church, which is His body, the fullness of Him who fills all in all (Ephesians 1: 22). Romans 8: 31-39.*

The more we adopt a conscious and deliberate attitude of obedience in seeking God's will for us it is with more ease that this communication flows. We train the senses to the unseen, while at the same time utterly rejecting any pagan attempt to blend truth with falsehood. *(1st Timothy 4: 6-10)* Here is one small example of how this works in the practice of deliverance and cleansing of place.

A couple had a rental home occupied by people buying and selling drugs. They had no idea what was going on until the drug addicted young people pulled up stakes and moved their operation. I was asked to pray over the property. I expected that she would pray with me, but she was so disturbed by the condition of the interior of the house that she left me to evaluate what repairs would be needed. And this was actually God's plan. He had something to say and I needed to hear it.

Bible, blessed water and salt in hand I began to pray against what I assumed would be the primary strongholds. When I got to the kitchen I stopped in my tracks. I was given a vision. I imagined the room painted fresh and clean. I saw the owner making breakfast at the stove and her husband coming in the door.

Then, God revealed something. He wanted my deliverance prayers focused in an entirely different area that centered on these two people; husband and wife. As I stood in the kitchen and pondered this vision, the Holy Spirit revealed something more. A demonic infestation commissioned by unholy prayers of agreement, spells and incantations had centered on making any who lived there physically ill. This infestation had been present through multiple occupants of the property.

How did I know this? God spoke to my spirit and I listened. Then I asked my Savior, Jesus Christ, if what I was hearing was the truth; testing what was revealed. The Holy Spirit said, "yes, this is right." I then believed what I heard from God and Jesus guided my next steps. Sound too simple? *Now we have received, not the spirit of the world, but the Spirit who is from God, so that we may know the things freely given to us by God, which things we also speak, not in words taught by human wisdom, but in those taught by the Spirit, combining spiritual thoughts with spiritual words (1st Corinthians 2: 12, 13).*

I decided to walk the property because I needed to test whether the infestation was invited and fixed after the house was built or was it part of the land and therefore regional to the neighborhood. More revelation was needed and having this knowledge would inform next steps. God revealed that the primary demonic infestation was within the house itself.

All of us are wired to receive messages from the unseen realm. When we read scripture it is often the case that a passage we've read many times before suddenly takes on new meaning, aligned perfectly to the challenge we are facing.   After a long period of seeking God in prayer we may experience an epiphany and have a clear and detailed plan for what we should do.   When sudden tragedy strikes, many Christians have remembered whole verses from scripture which they had not necessarily memorized. Along with the five senses we could consider an additional superfluity of other senses which allow us to hear from God.   The prophet Micaiah was given a glimpse into how this works. God had used Micaiah as Ahab's conscience. In this role of prophet he was hated and imprisoned by the evil duo of Jezebel and Ahab. And yet, God restrained Ahab from taking his life.   Micaiah was Ahab's very last chance. This is the vision seen by Micaiah and expressed out of a significant prophetic gifting.

After predicting defeat in battle Micaiah was given this glimpse of a transaction which transpired in heaven as warrior angels were dispatched. We also see that defeated demons, working through human beings, are revealed as used and controlled by the mighty power of God. ***Micaiah said, "Therefore, hear the word of the Lord. I saw the Lord sitting on His throne, and all the host of heaven standing on His right and on His left (2nd Chronicles 18: 18.)***

From his waking vision these are the instructional details that we can glean from what Micaiah describes to Ahab. Try to see it. ***The Lord said, 'Who will entice Ahab king of Israel to go up and fall at Ramoth-gilead?' And one said this while another said that. Then a spirit came forward and stood before the Lord and said, 'I will entice him.' And the Lord said to him, How? He said, 'I will go and be a deceiving spirit in the mouth of all his prophets.' Then He said, You are to entice him and prevail also. Go and do so. (2nd Chronicles 18: 19-21). Also 1st Kings 22: 20-22***

We cannot be effective in deliverance if we won't hear what the Holy Spirit reveals and then boldly share it with those who need to understand how to stand for their own freedom. In the exercise of visionary gifts we are operating in the unseen realm; we are learning to see with the ***eyes of our heart.   ...that the God of our Lord Jesus Christ, the Father of glory, may give to you a spirit of wisdom and revelation in the knowledge of Him (Ephesians 1: 17).*** Read the entire passage.

Ask God to prepare you to understand with discerning insight and revelation His word regarding intercession, miracles, healing, deliverance, exorcism, prophecy and the other spiritual gifts. Nothing substitutes for reading scripture. Nothing! By it Jesus Christ will manifest in your life in blessing, glory, wisdom, thanksgiving, honor, power, and strength. ***(Revelation 7: 12)***

Amen! *For I would have you know, brethren, that the gospel which was preached by me is not according to man. For I neither received it from man, nor was I taught it, <u>but I received it through a revelation of Jesus Christ</u> (Galatians 1: 11).* Pray for and expect these revelations. *And do not be conformed to this world, but be transformed by the renewing of your mind, so that you may prove what the will of God is, that which is good and acceptable and perfect (Romans 12: 2). Also Colossians 2: 8-15*

Nowhere is it proclaimed in scripture that supernatural impartations from God stopped after Christ's death and resurrection; nor after Pentecost. He created us, gave us this wonderful innate capability to powerfully communicate in spirit, the means by which we fellowship, the conveyance of visions, dreams, revelations. Jesus said: *"God is spirit and those who worship Him must worship in spirit and truth" (John 4: 24). ...but I will go on to visions and revelations of the Lord. I know a man in Christ who fourteen years ago – whether in the body I do not know, or out of the body I do not know, God knows – such a man was caught up to the third heaven (2nd Corinthians 12: 1b, 2).*

CHAPTER FIVE

HOW DO I KNOW? PROOF IN THE PUDDING!

"Till at his second bidding darkness fled, Light shone, and order from disorder sprung." -- John Milton

The most frequent search that gets people to my blog is some version of a question about discerning spirits. How do I know if I have this gift; what if I'm seeing or sensing spirits?

When Francis MacNutt was asked a similar question about healing he said, "you have the gift of healing if people are healed when you pray for them." The same is true of that God-given ability to discern spirits.

Jesus never said, at any time, to stop casting out demons. The early church did this on a regular basis and by example Jesus modeled this practice. *At that very time He cured many people of diseases and afflictions and evil spirits; and He gave sight to many who were blind (Luke 7: 21).* Jesus taught his apostles. Then He commissioned the seventy. *The seventy returned with joy, saying "Lord even the demons are subject to us in Your name" (Luke 10:17).*

From that time to now, some are appointed to operate in those spiritual gifts that define a deliverance calling. In the triumphant authority of Jesus, without fear, believers have authority to cast out demons.

Therefore, if anyone is in Christ, he is a new creation; the old has gone, the new has come! All this is from God, who reconciled us to himself through Christ and gave us the ministry of reconciliation (2nd Corinthians 5: 17, 18).

Deliverance is a ministry of reconciliation. It frees people to love Jesus. It enables sufferers to be strengthened so that a calling that has previously eluded may be embraced. *That He would grant you, according to the riches of His glory, to be strengthened with power through His Spirit in the inner man (Ephesians 3: 16).*

Deliverance has always required that we understand the need for freedom in the context of what individuals have suffered. In an act of warfare, the practice of deliverance wrests territory, under satanic control or influence, and breaks the fetters of bondage. *For He rescued us from the domain of darkness, and*

45

transferred us to the kingdom of His beloved Son, in whom we have redemption, the forgiveness of sins (Colossians 1: 13).

Believers that have a past history of exposure to the occult and been hurt by satanic agendas, may emerge with a powerful and significant gift of discernment. An example can be seen in the testimony of, Bill Bean. Past generations of Bill's family had been involved in the occult. This opened the door for satan to have legal access to future generations. Bill believes that his family was drawn to take up residence in a haunted house, infested by demons and evil spirits. He honed his skills in the crucible of terrible suffering and at thirteen, after trusting Christ, cast these demons, which materialized before him, from his home.

Many satanic devices may continue to linger in our lives operating out of submerged trauma and hidden or more obvious addictive sins, but also because of the sophisticated barrage of subliminal controls over which few have a conscious awareness. As they say, "garbage in, garbage out." Through the ministry of reconciliation we begin a process of being equipped to serve. Those who have a gift of discerning spirits may benefit from specially targeted training to give them the tools and understanding of what the word of God teaches. I like the training provided by Ken and Sylvia Thornberg from Freedom Encounters. www.freedomencounters.com.

Ken Thornberg points out that many churches don't know how to respond to SRA victims. On the one hand they want to deny that Satanic Ritual Abuse is real. On the other they are overwhelmed by the scope and broken condition of these victims. When the usual methods don't work, they are bewildered and feel their own faith threatened. Churches may end up blaming the victims so that they have an excuse to push these people away or pass them onto another church or therapist. This blame shifting is common because these broken people usually have few, if any, resources and, until delivered and healed present with overwhelming problems.

Wanting to encourage pastors to work in this area, Ken Thornberg describes what for him was, *"a long road to discovery"* taking what God has taught him to a place where any SRA victim can be helped. Partnering with a psychologist he began working with SRA victims at a time when few others were operating in this area. Ken says that many of these people, regardless of the severity... *"no matter what kind of programming, no matter how many rituals they've been through in the flesh or astral, I can guarantee them that in Christ they will be set free."*

While some are frightened by the profound changes that come with adopting freedom in Jesus Christ, Ken says: *"Most SRA's* would do anything to be free; they've always been the victim and never had an opportunity to be in control." Ken believes that if churches can step into effective ministry in this area some of those they've helped will stay and transform these churches. *"An average SRA survivor has gifts that the average believer does not have. They have discernment that is off the charts and many have spiritual sight. Churches not only don't know what to do with this, they don't know what spiritual sight is."*

If you have a gift of discerning spirits there could be little doubt that you are called to be a warrior; an officer in the church militant. **For though we walk in the flesh, we do not war according to the flesh, for the weapons of our warfare are not of the flesh, but divinely powerful for the destruction of fortresses (2nd Corinthians 10: 3, 4).** This verse goes on to identify where many demonic infestations set up. Even as we are casting demons out of a situation and sending them to the throne of God for immediate judgment... to be cast into the abyss never to be heard from again, we are doing battle against fields of satanic blindness, devices and various kinds of curse-ties. **We are destroying speculations and every lofty thing raised up against the knowledge of God, and we are taking every thought captive to the obedience of Christ... (2nd Corinthians 10: 5).**

Too often this verse is not applied to ourselves. Because of the times in which we live it's important to understand how often we are subjected to attempts at mind control. It takes a commitment to keep ourselves free from programming that invites us to forsake the tenets of a Biblical faith. **...and we are ready to punish all disobedience, whenever your obedience is complete (2nd Corinthians 10: 6).**

Many with this gift of discerning spirits may be drawn to isolate. This is a primary way that satan opposes us. The writer of Hebrews instructs: **Let us hold fast the confession of our hope without wavering, for He who promised is faithful; and let us consider how to stimulate one another to love and good deeds, not forsaking our own assembling together, as is the habit of some, but encourage one another; and all the more as you see the day drawing near (Hebrews 10: 22-25).**

The Prophet Daniel became a prisoner of war as a teenager during the Babylonian captivity. Along with three other Hebrew boys he was singled out to serve the king and by God's providence was force-fed instruction in the dark arts; the so called mysteries of the Chaldeans. These mysterious teachings were the stuff of satanic rites, spells, curses, and practices handed forward from the Tower of Babel. Even if not all these occult teachings were destroyed in the burning of the library at Alexandria, Egypt we would still have them today. Satan has always preternaturally communicated via demons, to those human-slaves chained by sin and occult practice. This same content can be seen in the paganism of the modern world. Nothing much changes. ***Woe to those who drag iniquity with the cords of falsehood, and sin as if with cart ropes (Isaiah 5: 18.) Woe to those who call evil good, and good evil; who substitute darkness for light and light for darkness; who substitute bitter for sweet and sweet for bitter (Isaiah 5: 20).***

The conflicts between good and evil are not always what we envision them to be. Satan is a crack addict on steroids, obsessive-compulsive legalist. The ropes and chains of such bondage inform the complicated labyrinth of what gives power to any satanically fueled agenda. Demons and evil spirits must operate within the death-grip of these legalistic scripts.

Fallen evil cannot conceive of grace. To the extent that we know the enemy so that our prayer life is informed as an intercessory force that crosses all divides to reach heaven and impact destiny on planet earth, grace and the love from which grace flows, cannot be entirely grasped by us. And yet His Holy Spirit fills us and resides within us. It is the grace nature of Jesus Christ working through us, His presence within us that makes possible a ministry of reconciliation via deliverance. Deliverance frees us to truly and fully repent. The walls are gone, the blindness lifts, damaging – joy stealing scripts are shattered.

The Light shines in the darkness, and the darkness did not comprehend it (John 1: 5). He is clothed with a robe dipped in blood and His name is called the Word of God (Revelation 19: 13). ...and the sword of the Spirit which is the Word of God (Ephesians 6: 17b).

Satan is not creative and cannot create. For this reason the methods and practices are predictable and have not changed throughout time. ***That which has been is that which will be, and that which has been is that which will be done. So there is nothing new under the sun (Ecclesiastes 1: 9).*** This is because God alone is the architect of all creation. ***He was in the beginning with God. All things came into being through Him, and apart from Him nothing came into being that has come into being (John 1: 2, 3).***

As a captive in a foreign land God allowed Daniel this exposure and testing so that in the crucible of holding onto his faith and what he knew to be true he would have learned to defend his sensibilities and his mind from preternatural onslaughts and temptations. This

48

is a learned skill. Being saved, transferred to the kingdom of light, immediately arms us. But now an informed proactive response and partnership is required. To take up the battle ready weapons and tools of our fight does not arrive by osmosis. We train the mind, we train the body. Laying sin aside we seek to be more like Jesus and less like our very lost, previous-self. *1st Corinthians 9: 19-27; Hebrews 12: 1-3.* Schooled in his Hebrew faith Daniel took a literal and committed view of God's admonition delivered through Moses: *And remember, never pray to or swear by any other gods. Do not even mention their names (Exodus 23: 13b). "You shall have no other gods before Me (Exodus 20: 3).* God says... *The sorrows of those who have bartered for another god will be multiplied; I shall pour out their drink offerings of blood, nor will I take their names upon my lips Psalm 16: 4.* Also *1st Corinthians 10: 20.*

Daniel understood that by God's foreknowledge he had arrived in the court of a foreign king for a divine purpose. The same is true of you. Look about and take stock. By sovereign and intentional plan, within the juxtaposed confluence of personal choice, you navigate a temporal life that will be lived once and only once on planet earth. *And inasmuch as it is appointed for men to die once and after this comes judgment (Hebrews 9: 27).*

You are so very important to God. *The Lord replied, "If you return to me I will restore you so you can continue to serve me. If you speak words that are worthy, you will be my spokesman. You are to influence them, do not let them influence you! They will fight against you like an attacking army, but I will make you as secure as a fortified wall. They will not conquer you for I will protect and deliver you. I, the Lord have spoken! Yes, I will certainly keep you safe from these wicked men. I will rescue you from their cruel hands (Jeremiah 15: 19-21).*

The attacking army God referred to as he spoke these words to his assigned prophet refers as much to the evil spirits as to men used by evil spirits. And God says to us, his daughters and sons, just as he said to Jeremiah that He... *"will protect and deliver you."*

The Chaldean priests were imbued by satanic, preternatural power. They were feared and respected because what they offered was real, and not, as some would like to think today, mere ignorant superstition. These teachings, which early Chaldean sects practiced, were exported to Egypt. *But the magicians of Egypt did the same with their secret arts...* Moses confronted these

49

powerful mages when God sent him to free the Hebrew people. God equipped Moses as both an exorcist and a miracle worker and Aaron as a prophet-spokesperson with the gift of exhortation. *(Exodus 7: 1).*

These mages (wizards and warlocks), had aligned themselves with pagan gods and behind these thrones of misguided worship were demons operating as vehicles of satanic destruction, able to imitate many of the miracles performed by Moses. *...and Pharaoh's heart was hardened, and he did not listen to them, as the Lord had said (Exodus 7: 22).*

The purpose of any miracle, in the words of Moses, is *...that you may know that there is no one like the Lord our God (Exodus 8: 10b).* Finally, all that Pharaoh had at his disposal, all the magicians, astrologers, sorcerers, and clairvoyants; all practitioners of the dark arts were no match for the one true God of the universe. The Egyptians finally had to admit a supreme, supernatural power greater than anything they practiced. Faced with the limitations of demonic power at work through human partnerships they admitted; *Then the magicians said to Pharaoh, "This is the finger of God." But Pharaoh's heart was hardened and he did not listen to them as the Lord had said (Exodus 8: 19).*

It is no effort for God to cast out demons, but in this description of Pharaoh's heart being "hard" and calloused we see the dual partnership between demonic activity and the entrenched stronghold of human will. Those who practice deliverance must be on the lookout for these partnerships which often masquerade as something other than what they are. It can be very difficult for human beings to admit they are wrong, to reverse course and see that what they've committed to isn't working. In playing God or refusing reconciliation man makes a futile attempt to defy and override the inherent powerlessness of the human condition.

Pharaoh strikes us as a dangerous fool. He is so accustomed to playing at being god that his assaultive actions and worship of self-will, self over God, over rides any inclination to act in the best interests of his people, or even himself. Wherever possession is a reality there is always the micro and then the macro strategy. In Pharaoh's case the demonic infestation is under satanic assignment to keep the Hebrew people from returning to the land in fulfillment of God's promises. It is from this people, needing to stay separate and apart as a people group from whom the Messiah and Savior would be born into a lost and dying world.

Some might say that this particular Pharaoh of history displays traits of classic narcissism. I would go further and assert that Pharaoh was also Ambulatory Possessed and therefore a demonically sanctioned psychopath.

Jesus said, *But if I cast out demons by the finger of God, then the kingdom of God has come upon you (Luke 11: 20).* To further make the point: *Truly, truly, I say to you, he who believes in Me, the works that I do, he will do also; and greater works than these he will do; because I go to the Father (John 14: 12).* Read the entire passage.

The Chaldeans studied astrology and astronomy. They based their occult beliefs and practices on a mix of science and special knowledge preternaturally conveyed by demons. There is no doubt that deliverance and exorcism is needed today. As a slave Daniel survived in the courts of four kings and two invasions. He could not have done so without a powerful gift of discerning spirits. He did this via an attuned ability to sense battles in the unseen realm which informed his prayer life and allowed the Lord to disclose needed information. Sometimes this veil between the material world and the unseen world fell away as in *Daniel 10: 10-21*.

Daniel was also an astute reader of those demons assigned to work through people. In the case of the Chaldean priests who had given themselves over to sorceries, channeling, enchantments, teleporting, curses, hexes and spells he would have been aware of the alien presence of demons living within and operating through the bodies of these revered mages whom he came into contact with on a regular basis. I'm convinced that Daniel converted some of these lost souls to faith in the greater power of Yahweh. We do know from scripture that on more than one occasion they conspired to kill Daniel and his cohort. When, you and I get to heaven we'll look back from eternity and see what today can only be imagined.

Daniel never converted to the Neo-Babylonian ways. Nor are we to be converted to any pagan and new age mingling of what satanic assignment thrusts in our direction. To be so marginalized is to commit a dire sin from which we need deliverance and forgiveness. Daniel did not allow anything he was exposed to from the Chaldeans to corrupt his unshakable faith in God. By divine wisdom Daniel interpreted dreams and received prophetic revelations from God. He recorded significant and detailed prophesies, some of which are yet to be fulfilled.

When the religious church claims that people do not need deliverance from evil spirits and that physical health is never tied to sin, or that prophecy is no longer needed or relevant we might ask where in the New Testament this is stated. Scripture and verse it cannot be quoted because it isn't there. Only via a lot of word soup and significant religious bias and referencing other books can any true believer arrive at these dead conclusions which serve satan far more than they do God. *But when He, the Spirit of truth,* *comes, He will guide you into all the truth; for He will not speak on His own initiative, but whatever He hears, He will speak; <u>and He will disclose to you what is to come</u> (John 16: 13).*

The Lord Jesus Christ knew we would stumble over the words in John 16: 13-15. Read the entire passage now. If we really believed Jesus' words we would be convicted to radically change the manner and frequency of prayer. If we really understood that divine revelation wasn't just for the past or the future, but for today, we would truly feel the joy of knowing Him in greater intimacy, in the personal and fluid expression of ministry. We would all be intercessors.

Jesus makes clear that disclosures, revelations, and impartations occur as the norm and not the exception. ***<u>He will disclose to you what is to come</u>. He will glorify Me, <u>for He will disclose it to you.</u> All things that the Father has are Mine; therefore I said that <u>He takes of Mine and will disclose it to you</u> (John 16: 14, 15).***

Do you get it? God will disclose to you revelation that you wouldn't otherwise have. It could be something as simple as a catch in your spirit that moves you to act or alerts you to a problem with your children. It could be something as momentous as a waking vision. Your job is to listen and see with the eyes of your heart. To develop the confidence of trusting Jesus to act on what His Spirit is communicating on a daily basis. Sharpen the eyes of your heart to receive in faith what cannot be, at least now, explained. God is the champion of us exercising the tools and gifts that allow us to operate in the sphere of his glory and power. No spiritual gift could or would contradict the glory of His design.

I wasted a lot of time denying certain gifts. I let a lot of poor decisions get in the way of my working within the sphere of His calling. I don't want that delay to impact your life. At some point we just have to decide it's time to bring momentum to our calling, whatever that calling happens to be. ***Then the Lord said to Moses, "Why are you crying out to me? Tell the people to get moving!" (Exodus 14: 15).***

CHAPTER SIX

KIND OF HOMESICK

My first real memory of realizing the differences between the satanic preternatural realms in conflict with God's supernatural realm and other dimensions coexisting parallel to the material world came as I headed down town with twenty five cents in my pocket. At the News Store, five nickels would buy five candy bars. This disclosure pretty much dates me.

My mother had a friend who would stay in our lives through much of my childhood. Even after my mother passed away this woman would continue to cast a toxic shadow over my life and perhaps to a lesser degree that of my siblings. Not until I did the work of forgiving her, which required counseling, was I free from the satanic imprint of this woman's dysfunction. I don't recall what incident led me to flee the house that day, but as I turned off Fletcher and walked down Church Street I called out to the God I didn't know with every fiber of my being for some kind of justice. I was ready to lose hope and I felt the threat of this loss as a dangerous infringement and potential death of some part of me that was human. I recall so clearly the emotional angst of that moment, so frustrated that I was beyond tears, but lacking the appropriate words to describe my state.

Children are very attached to this concept of fairness. They start life as right-fighters and then with maturity learn to negotiate the boundaries and limits of what can and cannot change. My cry that day was, "doesn't anyone care." As the daughter of a mother with a narcissistic personality disorder I was about to accept that they didn't.

As this primitive outrage erupted I felt an evil spirit-being reach for that soft place of my heart to make it hard and bitter. As I tensed and resisted I felt the unfathomable depth of the sky above and a great comfort descend. In that moment I came to realize that there was a counterpoint to the evil extreme of emotional neglect. This was God. The God of my Catholic faith was real. Was God also knowable? I experienced the invitation.

I had a good friend who has now passed on to heaven who grew up under satanic ritual abuse in a home that was utterly evil. My experiences compared to hers were the difference between an immature Shirley Temple and a consciously evil Cruella de Vil.

Despite the emotional damage that was done and all the obstacles she had to overcome, including ongoing therapy for integrating alter personalities, she managed to finish college and have a profession where she gave back to others in significant ways. Her faith in Jesus Christ and His love was a healing reality of which she was vividly conscious.

She told me that the turning point in her childhood came as she was being raped in a graveyard. She saw an angel who spoke to her and told her that she would have justice and a different life. Frank McCourt, who wrote the award winning book, *Angela's Ashes,* described the angel on the stair. This visitation from heaven and the knowledge that he was watched over by God contributed to Frank surviving horrible deprivation.

The miracle of what I experienced that day got me by until Jesus Christ revealed Himself more fully at age twenty three. Because of that experience of God's nearness that day some dangerous ways that I had been acting out came to an abrupt end. In my book *Wood's End* I gave the fictional character of Jared Shiel a similar visionary experience on the streets of North Adams, Massachusetts which just as profoundly altered his course.

As I grew older I sometimes wondered what part of me was so damaged that the filters which existed for others were not there for me. I've come to believe that I inherited this propensity to experience the unseen world in more overt ways than what might be called normal. I know that satan planned to use this to expand his kingdom, but God, the Ancient of Days, Jesus Christ my Savior and Lord had other ideas. Even before I was born I was marked as His. *You have enclosed me behind and before, and laid Your hand upon me. Such knowledge is too wonderful for me; it is too high, I cannot attain to it (Psalm 139: 5, 6).*

What many that are adept at discerning spirits have in common is early life experiences where for the sake of survival it was necessary to read the subtext of any given situation and, when possible, remove oneself to safety. Others just have this gift. They haven't honed it in the flux and pain of a dangerously lived childhood, but God has given this ability. Others have inherited this propensity to discern spirits as first, a generational curse and then, once saved and covered by the blood of Jesus Christ, a godly blessing. I fall into this last category.

I opened myself to faith in God when as a little girl I sang the song, "Away in a Manger," which became a holiday favorite throughout my childhood. Drawn by the Holy Spirit I believed the words. *Be near me Lord Jesus, I ask thee to stay, close by me forever and love me I pray!* Even today I can be ambushed by tears when I hear this song. We can certainly see the satanic agenda in getting Christmas pageants banned from public schools.

An understanding of God shifted into a new level of awareness at the funeral of my Irish grandfather. It was here that I felt the first call of God to embark on a path of knowing Him better. My grandfather, Patrick Clair, was born in Liscannor, County Clare, Ireland. After he came to the United States as a young man he worked for the railroad and later lived with his youngest daughter and her family.

His leaving Ireland was facilitated by his eldest sister Winifred Clair Bagley who settled in western Massachusetts. Winifred's daughter wrote a wonderful memoire of her mother's experience as a young immigrant. I regret that I didn't know him better because later in life I developed an interest in Irish history and began work on a yet uncompleted novel on Ireland called, *Clachan Maze*.

I have to this day a clear and vivid memory of walking up to the casket and peering into my grandfather's face. At that moment I was struck by a powerful revelation which I experienced as an enduring sense of loss for the human being that was now beyond my reach to ever know well. And then there was something more that I felt. Something awakened within and stirred the first awareness of what must lie beyond the grave because I wondered where my grandfather was. I made a connection between the spirits I had awareness of active in certain circumstances, and my grandfather no longer being at home to his body.

God did not leave me to sort this out alone. A drop of truth settled over the eyes of my heart and rose up in me as an impartation which then became conviction. Patrick Clair was not in this unseen spirit world which sometimes crossed paths with mine. What's more, the dangerous parts of this spirit world no longer had access to him. He was irrefutably gone. But, gone where? I felt a burning curiosity to know and in that moment, when for me the abstract of death became knowing, I felt prodded, deeply stirred, and even called by something unseen (the Holy Spirit) that made me aware of a lack, a void, and even an emptiness that existed in me.

I sometimes assign fictional characters, in one form or another, this same experience of confronting death. Although it doesn't start out as intentional it seems that in the writing I reaffirm the vast significance of that watershed moment when the desire for God to fill a void in my life was deeply felt and acknowledged by a lost little girl. As I struck out on life I would seek to have this void filled in counterfeit ways that resulted in sin.

As I prepared to turn away from the casket, with the combined scent of carnations and roses rising up to sting my nostrils, there were tears in my eyes. I knew that God was real. There was an afterlife, perhaps a more important real existence beyond the day to day despair of my early life and I felt a preternatural pull to be there. That sentiment was not new to me. I would entertain suicidal thoughts and feelings for much of my youth and some of my adulthood and not until I experienced deliverance for myself, many years after my salvation, did I truly experience freedom from the demonic tentacles' of this stronghold.

The common thread of what many of us who have struggled with very early suicidal thoughts and feelings have in common is a narcissistic parent. If someone presenting for deliverance tells me that they have attempted suicide and been controlled by these feelings I want to know if there has been proximity to such a personality, system, or cult.

It was very difficult for me to call evil, evil. From an early age, for the sake of health, I was challenged to navigate the dynamics of evil in a context that was beyond my maturity level to understand. How is it possible to both love and profoundly distrust someone whom we need and count on for life? Many of my early mistakes stemmed from anxiety over abandonment; losing or alienating a mother whom I simultaneously loved and feared, but admired for her many talents and dynamic personality.

As a little girl, it would have been dangerous to confront her. Not only did I not have the words, I didn't have the emotional or intellectual sophistication.

It was from my mother that I inherited this porous barrier between the material world and the spirit world. She knew that I had this ability and later, after I became a Christian, she shared with me some of her own experiences. I needed and received deliverance from these attachments which were undermining God's desire to use me more fully.

One of my family members is offended each time I speak the truth about having been impacted by a narcissistic personality in the formative years of my life. I'm sorry for this, but the fact is I fought too hard and too long for the freedom and deliverance to acknowledge, speak, and emotionally heal from certain inherited and preternaturally constructed strongholds. I will never return to that unhealthy place of refusing honesty so as to appease fantasy.

Secrets in any family become strongholds and in the end will serve no good purpose. The coping mechanisms that allow us to survive abuse as children do not serve us well as adults. This is because satan camps on trauma and wounding and seeks to strangle or stunt the growth and strength of what is new in Christ. And thus an understanding of deliverance after salvation is very important.

Those who work in the restoration ministry of exorcism and deliverance must strive for a personal honesty and I believe, need to experience deliverance for themselves. Without personal deliverance effectiveness will be hampered. If demons are allowed to speak, prior to or during deliverance, they will bring up painful, even shameful memories and the degree to which you have been healed is the degree to which you will stand and reject these attacks. When God forgives us we are entirely forgiven. He has removed our sins as far as the east is from the west and we are free indeed (*Psalm 103*). Jesus said, *"If you continue in My word, then you are truly disciples of Mine; and you will know the truth, and the truth will make you free (John 8: 31b, 32).*

If you've asked for forgiveness, but do not feel forgiven you need deliverance. If you are in bondage to habits you can't break you also need deliverance, whatever those habits, indulgences and patterns of practice happen to be. This could be anger, misplaced rage, overeating, and compulsions to gossip, chronic laziness, fear of legitimate and needed confrontation or whatever life consuming practice impedes faith and steals joy. Believers that have trouble sleeping and are perpetually sleep deprived also need deliverance.

We cannot heal from what we won't acknowledge. I personally think that the absence of infant bonding due to neglect opened the door for such a destructive early stronghold in my life. Coupled with that thin barrier between me and the unseen world, but for grace I would not have survived the early years of my life. It wasn't that I found Jesus, but that He found me. Over and over again He came knocking. I sometimes heard and I sometimes didn't. *And we know that God causes all things to work together for good to those who love God, to those who are called according to His purpose (Romans 8: 28).*

As long as I live on planet earth I must continually commit to the work of confronting my shortcomings. In this practice we are all in the same boat. *But if we judged ourselves rightly, we would not be judged (1st Corinthians 11: 31). Therefore, confess your sins to one another, and pray for one another so that you may be healed (James 5: 16). He who listens to the life giving reproof will dwell among the wise (Proverbs 15: 31).*

As part of a process I took stock and I'm still taking stock. I'll never forget the time a blog reader pointed out a self righteous tendency that was revealed in something I wrote. Not all criticism is valid, but this was and caused me to apologize and rewrite the offensive portion of this blog.

Healthy people ask for what they need and I had learned in my childhood not to expose my need; adopting a hard crust of detachment. In a world that weighs everything, with starts and closures, walls and cul-de-sacs there really is no dead-end; no real barrier to reconciliation with Christ. No matter the late hour grace offers the opportunity to do an about face. Jesus demonstrates the truth of this in the following parable.

"For the kingdom of heaven is like a landowner who went out early in the morning to hire laborers for his vineyard (Matthew 20: 1). Jesus goes on to tell us that the owner of the vineyard heads to the marketplace to hire laborers four times throughout the day; in the first, third, sixth and ninth hour. Each time a gracious invitation to work in the vineyard is extended and people, grateful for the wages that supports life, come.

Finally, at the very end of the day the landowner returns once more and offers another, final invitation to those who are going nowhere and have no heart for home. We could think of these lost souls as being on their death bed or in danger of being Fatally Possessed. They've already said "no" four times before, but here we see Jesus coming one last time. For whatever reason, in this last hour, these lost souls are willing to hear and respond. *And about the eleventh hour he went out and found others standing around; and he said to them, 'Why have you been standing here idle all day long? They said to him, 'Because no one hired us.' He said to them, 'You go into the vineyard too' (Matthew 20: 7).*

An hour later the day came to a close and dusk began to settle over the fields. *When evening came, the owner of the vineyard said to his foreman, 'Call the laborers and pay them their wages, beginning with the last group to the first' (Matthew 20: 8).*

Those who had worked longer naturally expected to be paid more and looked forward to a greater reward. In human logic this only seems fair. The last group invited to work would have hardly made it to the field, farm implement in hand and ready to join the rhythm of reaping, before the signal was given to return home.

In a response so contrary to human nature God gives us a picture of, not only grace, but eternal intent and destiny for lost souls. The landowner pays each person the same amount of money. The depths of God's love and mercy cannot be measured in the limitations of human reasoning. When told by those who worked longer that this isn't fair Jesus closes his parable with these words: *Is it not lawful for me to do what I wish with what is my own? Or is your eye envious because I am generous? So the last shall be first, and the first last (Matthew 20: 15, 16).*

God does not think as we do. He doesn't weigh and measure as we do. Jesus made this statement. *For this reason I say to you, her sins, which are many, have been forgiven for she loved much; he who is forgiven little, loves little (Luke 7: 47).*

Many of those in occult bondage are the least and their numbers are growing and sadly include many young people who grew up in churches that never addressed the toxic danger of occult topics. A church body has no authority to minister in this area if they fail to unashamedly acknowledge that there is an evil counter power in the preternatural clash of good over evil. *But as many as received Him, to them He gave the right to become children of God, even to those who believe in His name, who were born, not of blood nor of the will of the flesh nor of the will of man, but of God (John 1: 12, 13).*

Paul wrote that the grace given to him was... to *bring to light what is the administration of the mystery which for ages has been hidden in God who created all things; so that the manifold wisdom of God might now be made known through the church to the rulers and the authorities in the heavenly places. This was in accordance with the eternal purpose which He carried out in Christ Jesus our Lord, in whom we have boldness and confident access through faith in Him (Ephesians 3: 9-12).*

As human persons we do our best to take what we don't understand and reframe it in the context of the material world. Unless we truly acknowledge our relationship with what isn't seen we'll never be powerfully equipped to engage as we should in the great cosmic battle over a fallen planet.

God doesn't always answer prayer in the way we want or expect. Though we have fasted and prayed some people are not physically healed. This is the time that God is calling them home. Some that come to faith fall away or are delivered only to relapse back into sin;" *2nd Peter 2: 22.* How can we explain this? Regardless of the outcome we are called to proclaim that change is possible; Jesus is the answer. He proclaimed, *I have come as Light into the world, so that everyone who sees Me sees the One who sent Me (John 12: 45).* In obedience to a deliverance calling we carry this Light into dark places and when we do, evil flees.

Ezekiel's calling was to the house of Israel. Occult bondage was a prevalent societal imprint and influence. As a prophet Ezekiel grieved over the numbers of people that refused to turn back to Yahweh. God put this in perspective, letting Ezekiel know that He required, not a legalistic quota... no score sheet, but simple obedience. As a prophet and in the context of that calling, Ezekiel would speak the truth whether it was received or not and for this God would bless and protect His bond-servant.

God said: *As for them, whether they listen or not – they will know that a prophet has been among them. And you, son of man, neither fear them nor fear their words, though thistles and thorns are with you and you sit on scorpions; neither fear their words nor be dismayed at their presence, for they are a rebellious house. But you shall speak My words to them whether they listen or not for they are rebellious (Ezekiel 2: 5-7). Also Ezekiel 3: 17-19).*

Micah put this in simple terms. *He has told you, O man, what is good; and what does the Lord require of you but to do justice, to love kindness, and to walk humbly with your God (Micah 6:8).*

"I'm kind of homesick for a country to which I've never been before; no sad goodbyes will there be spoken, for time won't matter anymore..." Lyrics from: Beulah Land.

Paul expressed this yearning for his true heavenly home. *...we are of good courage, I say, and prefer rather to be absent from the body and to be at home with the Lord. Therefore we also have as our ambition, whether at home or absent, to be pleasing to Him (2nd Corinthians 5: 8, 9).*

For this is the love of God, that we keep His commandments; and His commandments are not burdensome. For whatever is born of God overcomes the world and this is the victory that has overcome the world – our faith (1st John 5: 3, 4). Matthew 11: 28-30.

CHAPTER SEVEN

THE PROPHET-EXORCIST

But also some of the Jewish exorcists, who went from place to place, attempted to name over those who had the evil spirits the name of the Lord Jesus, saying "I adjure you by Jesus whom Paul preaches" (Acts 19: 13).
What follows is the Biblical account of the seven sons of Sceva. Sceva was a Jewish High priest. His sons were minor celebrities. Whatever they did would have caught the attention of the populace. We don't know how many of these impetuous young men later came to faith in the one true Messiah, Jesus Christ. I like to think they all did. What we see demonstrated is that an aggrandized view of self, dependent on church tradition, is devoid of power in spiritual battle.

In the course of this attempted exorcism the primary demon spoke and said... *And the evil spirit answered and said to them, "I recognize Jesus, and I know about Paul, but who are you? And the man, in whom was the evil spirit, leaped on them and subdued all of them and overpowered them, so that they fled out of that house naked and wounded (Acts 19: 15, 16).*

From this account we understand that freedom can only be achieved by the power of Christ operating through a genuine and true faith. Luke, inspired by the Holy Spirit, singles out this account from so many that he would have witnessed and especially as he lived his faith in company with Peter, John, and Paul. As important as what actually happened, is the outcome that followed. *This became known to all, both Jews and Greeks, who lived in Ephesus; and fear fell upon them all and the name of the Lord Jesus was being magnified (Acts 19: 17.)*

That this event ushered in genuine revival is evidenced in the outcome. *Many also of those who had believed kept coming, confessing and disclosing their practices. And many of those who practiced magic brought their books together and began burning them in the sight of everyone; and they counted up the price of them and found it fifty thousand pieces of silver (Acts 19: 18, 19).*

We don't know what happened to the man who was possessed. Perhaps Luke returned to the house in question and performed a

61

true exorcism. Large numbers of lost people were brought to faith in Jesus Christ as a spotlight was shone on the counterfeit. Revival operates in concert with miracles through the ministry of reconciliation; exorcism, deliverance, and healing. *The night is almost gone, and the day is near. Therefore let us lay aside the deeds of darkness and put on the armor of light (Romans 13: 12).*

Luke's concluding word... *So the word of the Lord, was growing mightily and prevailing (Acts 19: 20).* Prevailing over darkness; Amen!

Paul made the point that the office of apostle would not end with the twelve as many denominations teach today. When he was accused of not being one of the original twelve and therefore not having the same authority as Peter and the others, Paul said: *The signs of a true apostle were performed among you with all perseverance, by signs and wonders and miracles (2nd Corinthians 12: 12).* Paul made this point not merely to defend his divine calling, but for the many that would come after him called to wear the supernatural mantle of an apostle. *God was performing extraordinary miracles by the hands of Paul, so that handkerchiefs or aprons were even carried from his body to the sick, and the diseases left them and the evil spirits went out (Acts 19: 11).*

Some people have this gift, but rarely is this gift nurtured and mentored, let alone recognized in the overburdened religious church. *Now you are Christ's body, and individually members of it. And God has appointed in the church, first apostles, second prophets, third teachers, then miracles, then gifts of healings, helps, administration, various kinds of tongues (1st Corinthians 12: 27, 28).*

A serious disconnect occurred as the various denominations denied the need for the role of exorcist in modern culture. Deciding that the visionary gifts were no longer needed and throwing the church out of balance by over emphasizing the safer, more easily controlled pastoral gifts, church bodies came to be influenced to a greater extent by cycling societal trends, looking more and more like the world. Adopting an out of balance reverence for science and analytics the material was elevated above scripture, forsaking the mystery and miracles of a true anointing to first recognize the degree of demonization and then to offer freedom to those in bondage in the practice of healing, deliverance, and exorcism.

One of the more tragic outcomes of this imbalance in churches is that many men and women, called to these areas, have left the church. They've done so because of conflicts with abusive church hierarchies which at the core level, were never going to forsake the bondage and lies of tradition for the truth and light of scripture. Consider how poorly many have been equipped to fight these battles by seminaries and denominational constructs which too often stand against the word itself; philosophizing the word of God.

Some have tragically walked away from a full time ministry and calling to discern spirits. They were not fulfilled in ministry because their calling was never recognized. Well meaning people tried to mold and indoctrinate them to conform and pattern visionary gifts to fit their show. It's a little like being adopted into a family that has no love for music and the arts. But in your DNA is stamped a creative passion whose song cannot be extinguished. ***Therefore do not throw away your confidence which has a great reward. For you have need of endurance, so that when you have done the will of God, you may receive what was promised (Hebrews 10: 35).***

Jeremiah was called to his visionary gifts during a difficult period of Hebrew history. ***"Before I formed you in the womb I knew you, and before you were born I consecrated you; I have appointed you a prophet to the nations" (Jeremiah 1: 5).***

Jeremiah is sometimes called the reluctant prophet. His honesty allows us to self-identify with the ambivalence that comes with all visionary gifts. Jeremiah expressed this deeply ingrained mandate to discern spirits in the context of his prophet responsibility as a destiny impossible to ignore. ***But if I say, I will not remember Him or speak anymore in His name, then in my heart it becomes like a burning fire shut up in my bones; and I am weary of holding it in, and I cannot endure it (Jeremiah 20: 9).***

Jonah is another example of a reluctant prophet. We cannot escape the fact that Jonah was both a prophet and an exorcist. He is an exorcist because he enters battle ready to stand for deliverance, for the souls of people who are so bound by satan that they are not seeking God. Not a one of those persons saved at Nineveh knew the one true God before Jonah showed up to do battle on their behalf. Oh yes, they knew of Him in the context of a known history of the Hebrew people. They would have been hurt by the deep patterns of sin which accompany occult practice, but they were not seeking the one true God. And yet, God showed up. ***"I was found by those who did not seek Me, I became manifest to those who did not ask for Me (Romans 10: 20b).***

Jonah did not flee from the threat of evil or from being in evil circumstances where occult practice brought to Nineveh a confluence of many demonic spirits and their virulent activity.

63

Jonah fled from the voice of God's demand and anointing to be what, with foreknowledge and plan, God created him to be. ***The word of the Lord came to Jonah the son of Amittai saying, "Arise, go to Nineveh the great city and cry against it for their wickedness has come up before Me." But Jonah rose up to flee to Tarshish <u>from the presence of the Lord</u> (Jonah 1: 1-3a).***

We read that the extreme wickedness of the people had come to the attention of God; not that they were crying out to God or seeking Him. It is the compassion we feel for hurting and lost people that draws us to minister. Many missionaries labor without seeing souls saved as prophet-exorcists before a generation or two later missionary-evangelists and teachers enter the picture. This was very much the case when the first English missionaries traveled to India and China; places with deep roots into demonic bondage and worship with satanic territorial imprint, infestation, and influence.

Jonah had an inherent sensitivity to perceive evil. His gift was to discern spirits; the demons which operated behind the thrones of pagan worship. We know from scripture that a generation later the entire city returned to their pagan ways, but we also know something of God's unchangeable grace-nature. The generation that lived the miraculous rescue and revival that took place in Nineveh were healed from the imprint, the infestation, and the influence through the calling of a prophet-exorcist. Many would have been led away to start new lives.

Nineveh is the only time in scripture that we read of an entire city being saved. We must note that before repentance could usher in revival there had to be a cleansing of place; a corporate exorcism. Sometimes people pray for healing and never consider that first they need to break the curses through deliverance. ***Then the people of Nineveh believed in God; and they called a fast and put on sackcloth from the greatest to the least of them (Jonah 3: 5).***

At each step Jonah was ambivalent. At no time did Jonah's inner conflict negate the miraculous outcome ordained by God. Reluctant obedience in heeding a divine calling is a good and valid place to start. God anointed Jonah, the reluctant prophet-exorcist and this anointing overrode every human wish to be free of who he was divinely empowered to be. God called Jonah's depression, anger. When Jonah expressed his feelings, even his disapproval, God replied: ***Should I not have compassion on Nineveh, the great city in which there are more than 120,000 persons who do not know the difference between their right hand and left hand, as well as many animals (Jonah 4: 11).***

One of the most remarkable features about the book of Jonah is who wrote it. Jonah wrote the book of Jonah. In these pages he shines a light on all his faults and failures. In doing so he invites accountability for himself and inspires the need for such in us. As he processed what happened, one can only imagine that this genuine commitment to personal honesty and accountability is the emergence of Jonah reconciling the strength and fruit of a visionary calling. First and foremost an exorcist; one called to those in bondage to satanic infestations, true of both the city and the people, the physical place and the invisible soul.

Exorcism is for those not seeking God. They don't recognize their profound and life stealing wretchedness, but by divine appointment they come to the attention of a deliverance or intercessory prayer team; perhaps even a Christian counselor, priest, or pastor. They are ignorant of what true faith can accomplish. We share the gospel both before and after the demons are banished to the throne of God for immediate judgment – cast into the abyss by the finger of God, never to be heard from again and with all backups and replacements likewise and immediately destroyed. (Words matter)

Deliverance is for those that know Jesus Christ. At some point they recognize a need for freedom. They may be harassed by demons. They may not experience victory over a pattern of practice that God convicts them of like gossip or withholding love from a spouse or a less favored child. They may be addicted or physically sick via satanic carrier elements set up in their bodies as a disease or infection.

Disease did not exist before the fall and so we know that when we pray for healing we must take into account the need for freedom from harmful carrier elements under preternatural assignment and given authority for whatever reason. We want to see every cell in the body cleansed and healed so that people can be restored to serving Jesus Christ in joy and intimacy. First deliverance and then healing.

Jonah's struggle to deny God's calling was a desire to have God on his terms. This path, if persisted in, brings grief to every believer and impacts subsequent generations.

What happened to Jonah? In **2ⁿᵈ Kings 14: 25** there is a reference to Jonah. By this we know that he went on to embrace his calling as prophet-exorcist; a man who discerned spirits and the demonic imprint of places with the God-given acuity of a visionary gift.

Fr. Malachi Martin in his book, *Hostage to the Devil (ISBN 0—06-065337-X; Copyright – Library of Congress)* tells the story of a Catholic priest who attempts an exorcism only to find that, despite an officially sanctioned vocation, he lacked a genuine faith and therefore had no authority. Only after coming to Jesus Christ in repentance was he able to return to lead a successful exorcism.

Luke 8: 26-39; Luke 9: 37-43; Matthew 15: 21-28 record examples of Jesus conducting exorcisms. Jesus instructs the demons to depart and they do; even from far off. This doesn't take days as the examples given in Martin's book. And yet, Jesus tells his followers that, "this kind" does not go out except by prayer and fasting. Read *Matthew 17: 21* in context. There was a need to build faith; sending up prayers to the throne of grace. We are told that fasting humbles our heart; bringing forth God's word. There is something to know – and in the context of Exorcism getting rid of any sin in our own lives well in advance of the actual exorcism – is part of our preparation in that sin stands as a barrier to hearing from God.

There is no simple superficial formula, but there is a learned process. For this we understand the importance of investigation and preparation; discerning the spirits so that we can be fully armed. *Hostage to the Devil* provides clinical and spiritual insight into the process of how people become possessed. Many people have been influenced by Martin's work, including M. Scott Peck and myself. The last and final toxic state of possession which I call Fatally Possessed, Fr. Malachi Martin called, Perfectly Possessed. I just didn't like the term perfect assigned to anything satanic.

People that are ambulatory possessed have seen sin atrophy choice as a God-given right and are severely limited in how they can cooperate. The practice and training taught by Ken and Sylvia Thornberg and offered to churches as an in-depth training program, are, I believe, highly effective for the day and age in which we currently live. www.freedomencounters.com

Jesus conducted the following exorcism from far off. A woman cries out, *"Have mercy on me, Lord, Son of David; my daughter is cruelly demon-possessed." But He did not answer her a word. And His disciples came and implored Him saying "Send her away, because she keeps shouting at us."*

We see that this woman is so desperate for help that she cares not at all for social decorum. This is more about Christ breaking preconceived notions; tearing down the lies, the delusional energy field of bias and ignorance in those that are observing this exchange. For the sake of His audience and the spotlight it shines on their lack of faith and failure to see what's important, Jesus reminds this mother... *"I was sent only to the lost sheep of the house of Israel."*

Now that she has Jesus' attention she experiences hope. Jesus is looking at her. This is a start. There is something about this look, and what is communicated that she knows is significant. He loves her. Jesus sees us and, nevertheless, He loves us.

The woman lays out her argument. I love this... how she doesn't give up; she intercedes laying all her heartache bare. Those observing may deride her further, but that's not the point. She'll take this risk, having already left her child and traveled to seek after Jesus. As always, Jesus will be found.

But she came and began to bow down before Him, saying, "Lord, help me!" And He answered and said, "It is not good to take the children's bread and throw it to the dogs." But she said, "Yes, Lord; but even the dogs feed on the crumbs which fall from their masters' table." Then Jesus said to her, "O woman, your faith is great; it shall be done for you as you wish." And her daughter was healed at once. (From: Matthew 15: 21-28)

Notice that deliverance and exorcism is healing. Notice also that parents have the authority to contend for children. God is grace.

CHAPTER EIGHT

ENERGY FIELDS of DELUSIONAL BLINDNESS

After all this I saw another angel come down from heaven with great authority, and the earth grew bright with his splendor. He gave a mighty shout, "Babylon is fallen – that great city is fallen! She has become the hideout of demons and evil spirits, a nest of filthy buzzards, and a den of dreadful beasts (Revelation 18: 1, 2).

There are different spirits which we encounter in deliverance. People with a gift for discerning these spirits can inform the team and process. If we are there for the deliverance of a person, this person's freedom and protection is our primary concern. We do not minister in deliverance and exorcism to satisfy our own curiosity or that of others. Clearly the sons of Sceva, of Acts 19 fame, on some level were testing the theory of Christ and that of Christ's exorcist, Paul. This would not be honoring to Christ, and does not serve the divine calling to which God has anointed us: To free a property, a person, or an organization.

There are intercessor's gifted for purposes of deliverance that are given glimpses into the unseen, which God allows for a purpose, and the person leading the deliverance team should be responsible for the decision on what to do with this information. Everything seen and discerned doesn't need to be shared. Not only can this harm the person who has courageously asked for help, but may additionally exploit their pain and trauma.

The Holy Spirit reveals, by supernatural impartation, how we should pray regarding what we may encounter and this often drives the investigative stage where we are exploring something about those who are being harmed, what kind of freedom is needed, what devices have been implanted, and then what aftercare will be provided. No matter how much preparation we do there will always be the unexpected. My father called it a "right hook."

The person needing freedom doesn't know everything and will most likely disclose something in the midst of deliverance not previously shared. When dealing with alters, you may find there is some information that part of this person knows, but which another part has no memory of. Think of experience as never really being lost. Experience is owned and understood in part, yet always fully present at some core level where language isn't present or where trauma has splintered off the painful threat of processing. It is necessary to understand this when praying for deliverance. It's also true that perpetrators controlling and abusing this person while young and vulnerable has programmed them, an implanted device, from which deliverance is needed. These devices can be thought of as curses which operate on an unconscious level; on auto-pilot.

Memory is tricky and complex; selective and mercurial. In preparation for deliverance, people share what they have consciously constructed in order to navigate life. Some of this is true, and some is false. Strategies that may have shielded the sufferer in childhood do not work in the real world for adults. These deflecting strategies become patterns of practice that are preternatural strongholds of delusional blindness which stand as barriers to healing.

We must never view all this in simplistic terms. Doing so results in blame-shifting toward the victim. A biased view of what should transpire based on superficial religious tradition and lack of knowledge of the enemy and his tactics, where we are in church history, results in spiritual abuse.

God designed human beings to adapt in order to survive. Only now it is time for deliverance and the kind of honesty that sets a person free. Deliverance should be seen as the catalyst to healing. Deliverance makes healing possible. This is what deliverance is all about. Never harsh, but caring, while accurately wielding the word of God in banishing forever whatever satanic assignment whether it be the generational curses, besetting sin, addictions, the hurtful patterns of behavior that harm self and others.

The need for aftercare is not an indicator that deliverance or healing has in any way failed. A deliverance ministry without aftercare is like a car without wheels. As the body of Christ, we must put this notion that we are above accountability to rest. Every effective program has built into it measures which provide objective feedback and this feedback begins with aftercare.

A few are miraculously and forever healed. They walk away and do just fine. For most, a foundational insight and understanding of themselves in the context of having been delivered and healed, in order to dislodge deeply embedded destructive scripts, are needed in aftercare.

Once the deliverance itself is over people may feel scared. What previously controlled their life is now gone. The former state was at least known and even predictable. Newly delivered people may be feeling the love of Christ for the first time. They are ambushed by intense emotion as they consider what it means to exercise autonomy; this new freedom in Christ. There may even be simple life skills which we take for granted, but that they, fighting for survival, were never organized enough to learn; managing money or keeping house. In the BBC series, *Lark Rise to Candleford*, we see Miss Lane re-parenting Mini who has suffered physical, mental, and spiritual abuse. This is the aftercare that builds trust and strength to which the church body is called.

Abuse victims may interpret this newness in Christ as being vulnerable. Risking love, receiving love has never been trusted and for good reason. We can see how valuable a healthy church body, understanding demonic and occult bondage would be to this ministry. Fellow believers that can speak encouragement and show Christ-love, offering prayer and fellowship, and Biblical teaching to replace the lie and fear scripts at times of setback are crucial to the ongoing process of restoration. All this and more comprises a church aftercare program.

Sadly, it must be said: If a church will have an aftercare program they must first open their hearts and minds to the need for deliverance, exorcism, and healing. They must first have a leader-pastor who will speak out against the occult in real Biblical terms.

Too many, well-meaning Christian leaders trade on dramatic stories under the guise of helping other people or showing financial donors that the program is successful. This is dangerous because premature expectations will push the person who has survived to meet performance scripts before they are ready and before they have learned healthy tools to navigate a new faith in Christ. Nothing shuts down the Holy Spirit faster than not being transparent and genuine. The abuser or the cult, the addiction or whatever life stealing bondage they have been delivered from, has trained these people to posture the lie that all is well. When memories or flashbacks surface they are, in the subtext of these damaging "religious expectations," encouraged to go right back to the "secret keeping" that has so robbed them of peace and kept them in bondage.

The subtext of what is conveyed is this: If they disclose ambivalence, admit they are struggling, or ask for help they are letting God down because they have, after all, been healed and delivered, and they owe these Christian believers a debt of gratitude. This has been the tragic undoing of many addicts. Having lived under threat, and being newly delivered, makes some especially vulnerable to relapse. They are fearful of undermining or disappointing the new support system that they've come to depend on. How tragic that well-meaning believers and Christian leaders interrupt the healing process, and see aftercare as evidence of God not working. This is where religious abuse picks up where satan left off, and opens the door to more bondage.

Those who have been delivered from horrific life trials and dangerous circumstances in a transforming miracle of God's grace need the time to determine what they will publicly share about past abuse. They need time to grow in Christ, learning to see God as a trusted Father and Savior. At some point, perhaps even immediately, some will want to share their testimony. They must never be told to share details that will make them vulnerable to more abuse.

What follows is an example of how we seriously undermine the health and interrupt the healing process when we have legalistic and inflexible expectations of how God will work. Jennifer used a couple of words I wouldn't have, but decided not to omit them, for reasons that should be obvious.

What happened to Jennifer was publically known in the community where she lived. It was common knowledge that her step-father had been arrested, stood trial, was convicted and went to prison. Jennifer's mother and grandmother shared too many personal details, with no thought for how she might later be impacted by their imprudent disclosures. This assuaged their guilt, but did nothing for twelve year old Jennifer who was lost in the tumult of their neediness.

After the trial and a brief period of court ordered counseling Jennifer's youth pastor asked her to share her testimony. By this time she was fourteen; shy and distrustful of people, but naturally engaging when standing before a microphone. It turned out that her aptitude for public speaking made her popular at area youth groups and Christian summer retreats and she began to travel with a youth choir as a speaker whose story galvanized every congregation.

When reading Jennifer's account notice her use of the term "switch." Abuse victims are practiced at using this tool of depersonalization when threatened. Many people have no awareness or insight into why they acted as they did and people observing them, unless they would discern the spirits operating, may remain blind. In Jennifer's case her church exploited her suffering and set her up for relapse. Some strategies that allow survival turn to bite us if we are not fully delivered. Unhealed trauma with no insight into how demons operate, become embedded strongholds from which deliverance is needed.

I asked if there was a wise older woman at her church who might have discerned, as a rational understanding of the dynamics of such abuse, Jennifer's suffering and stepped in to protect and mentor her ongoing recovery. I got a long answer. With her permission I turned on the tape recorder. In part, this is what she said.

"In the beginning I liked speaking. I got up there and it was like a switch was switched on and lots of people said that was great and for a while I thought, well, maybe it is. My mother and grandmother would drive me and afterwards we'd go to eat and being with my mother felt really, really good; having her to myself. Because he did everything he could to steal that and to make me think... and to make my mother think I was a bad child and only he understood me; he could help.

After the trail I thought, I didn't tell her everything, but now she knows and she still loves me. We'll get closer. But, that didn't happen. Sometimes she would coach me. She'd discuss it with the pastor and she'd say, don't say this, say this. If I cried or got carried away with a detail I'd been told not to tell about I would see my grandmother in the back of the church and she'd get up and leave. Then maybe for a week she'd act all, kind a, kind of mad. They liked the attention, but they didn't really want to know what happened to me; how what happened changed me forever. So there was this distance between me and the two people that were left after he was arrested. And it wasn't the same as before... when he was in the picture, but in some ways it was worse. My mother, she was my world. At fifteen, sixteen she was still my world. That's what I felt.

I ask a question. She answers and after a bit Jennifer continues her story.

So I had always feared losing my family, because you know, that bastard told me I would, but at first they rallied around me. It took a while for me to see that I still didn't have them. Not really. A lot of other girls came forward and told me what happened to them. I realized I wasn't alone and this felt good. But then a lot of the kids went back to school and talked about me. I wasn't ready to deal with that. Words hurt and I was very hurt. I started to feel like I was circus performing; a bare back rider with no clothes on, exposed and no protection. It was familiar; felt more and more like more of the same; you know... more abuse and stuck. Just stuck, only I didn't know enough to call it abuse. I had no idea then that I was entitled to privacy... that it might be okay to say I wasn't ready to talk about something; to say no, I'll share this, but not this and I won't lie so you can sleep at night. I was just pushed out into that circus ring to perform. Then there might be another few songs and maybe some other kid would share about arguing with their parents or drinking and I'd think. I wish I had your problems. There would be an invitation and we'd pack up and go home.

I know God used it. Some kids trusted Christ, but I started to feel responsible. Like I had no choice and it was me and not God that did that work and that was a lot of pressure... too much, really. And adults kept saying that. You're making a difference; you're brave, only I didn't feel brave. I knew I was saved, but I felt used and exploited. You know... A couple of years went by and I was getting very depressed only it crept up on me and I was performing; stuffing my feelings. I didn't know.

One day I just stopped caring about school and became just filled with rage every time my mother wanted to push me out there. She'd say, what's wrong? Why aren't you going to youth group; what about church and homework? And I'd just glare at her and lock my door. I just hated her. I mean I hated her for asking. Then she asked the pastor to call me and I hated him. Then my grandmother said she knew I'd back-step and let everyone down and no problem, I already hated her. My pain wasn't about me; it didn't belong to me. It was about them and how they used it.

I lived in a small town so I got paranoid. Thought I was being pointed at and trash-talked and I had no control over that and I hated and resented it. I knew that church was the place to feel safe in the love of God and I wished I could just go to another church and worship God and be anonymous. But by that time everything about life just sucked; seemed like too much trouble. For me, it was like... okay, it was like cut open the wound, but don't bleed anywhere near this house, this nice youth group or this pulpit. So I started not taking those calls. I made up excuses and then I'd flat out say no, and when they said, why not, what's wrong, like they really cared I'd scream and say none of your ____ business. That felt good. It felt honest. Rebellion felt honest.

I started doing drugs. Went from nada to heroin. Went out looking for it and weren't hard to find. It wasn't about punishing my mother and pastor. It was about not wanting to feel any more. I didn't care if I died. I knew I'd go to heaven so why shouldn't I? That's how sick I was; loving that needle. It went on for over a year. I overdosed twice. But that was my thinking. So, even though I knew Jesus had saved me and loved me, it was like I was saying to God, how do I get out of this deep hole I've been in since I was six? Why did you get me out only to push me in another, deeper hole? When do I get to be real? I couldn't win. It was no win."

We talk about addiction, about her mother and her pastor and legalistic churches in general. She talks about her step-father. She expresses anger that in half the time that she was abused the pedophile perpetrator was released from prison. Then we talk about where she is today. *God gave me a wonderful counselor who loved God. She wouldn't let me get away with blaming God or me for what happened that I couldn't control. There is nothing concealed that won't be revealed and that has comforted me. Today I hold onto the truth. Without that I go backwards."*

Therefore do not fear them, for there is nothing concealed that will not be revealed, or hidden that will not be known (Matthew 10: 26).

What happened to Jennifer? She went to rehab and then to a Christian counseling program for women where she stayed for eight months. She decided she needed distance from her mother and grandmother, church and town and today, isn't sure she will ever return home. Jennifer's mother traveled to where she was and together they had some shared counseling, which helped them both. Her grandmother refused to participate after Jennifer disclosed that she had revealed the abuse to her grandmother who failed to report her abuser and therefore failed to protect her.

Presently, Jennifer is on the campus of a Christian college. She knows she wants to work in the area of helping and protecting children, but is not yet sure what that will look like. She's waiting on God to tell her.

For any believer stuck in counseling with little change, deliverance will, most always jumpstart the counseling process. Too bad Christian counselors do not often take advantage of deliverance as an important component of a treatment plan. Still, counseling is not a substitute for aftercare; being loved by fellow believers, embraced by a healthy church body and learning the Biblical tools to walk in freedom. The isolation that was part of the fear script is the biggest threat to setback.

Truly, truly, I say to you, he who believes in Me, the works that I do, he will do also; and greater works than these he will do; because I go to the Father (John 14: 12). God wants to do these works. He wants to heal, restore, and deliver.

A good questionnaire, what level of occult involvement for example, tells us something about what we'll encounter, but it doesn't prepare the deliverance team for everything.

People who are easily shocked or highly emotional are not called to this ministry. **But in all these things we overwhelmingly conquer through Him who loved us. For I am convinced that neither death, nor life, nor angels, nor principalities, nor things present, nor things to come, nor powers, nor height, nor depth, nor any other created thing, will be able to separate us from the love of God,**

which is in Christ Jesus our Lord (Romans 8: 37-39).

Father God inspired the prophet Isaiah to speak for Him and in so doing let Isaiah know of the delusional and oppositional blindness that he would contend with throughout his life. Much of this is the political and religious territorial strongholds over which demons exercise imprint, infestation, and influence.

Isaiah was to speak the truth regardless of outcome. *He said, "Go and tell this people: Keep on listening, but do not perceive; keep on looking, but do not understand. Render the hearts of this people insensitive, their ears dull, and their eyes dim, otherwise they might see with their eyes, understand with their hearts, and return and be healed" (Isaiah 6: 9-10.)* Notice the connection between truth and healing.

A delusional, demonically assigned, oppositional blindness is always erected around people that are being used by satan and/or, around those that need exorcism or deliverance. No one is able to maintain power over others without the cooperation of these fallen entities that partner in actually occupying and working from within these energy fields. What was missed in Jennifer's family was that her mother, who had passively turned a blind eye to what was happening, also needed deliverance. One encounters this energy field in places, in circumstances, and around people.

If I had but one concept to get across to those who are called to discern spirits, it would be to consciously develop the ability to recognize these energy fields of delusional blindness. What is most often initially perceived is confusion. Learn to read what God is telling you. Pray as an exercise of exploration. Ask God for the truth and test the spirits. Then formulate a plan. *Beloved, do not believe every spirit, but test the spirits to see whether they are from God, because many false prophets have gone out into the world (1st John 4: 1).*

Beware of the false prophets, who come to you in sheep's clothing, but inwardly are ravenous wolves (Matthew 7: 15). Jennifer's step father was a ravenous wolf. He carefully selected the parent so he could groom the child to silently endure his abuse.

How do people become ravenous wolves? Answer: they partner with evil allowing the presence of demons and evil spirits to influence their thinking and/or to dictate and then control their actions. As this process develops unchecked, the energy fields take shape and grow in layered complexity.

How do we recognize false people? *You will know them by their fruits. Grapes are not gathered from thorn bushes nor figs from thistles, are they? (Matthew 7: 16).* Learn to read behavior and trust what the eyes of your heart are telling you. Take the time, to "know their fruits." Discerning spirits is not some nebulous, feelings based method of arriving at truth. Its use requires no tricks or artifice. Practice of the gift alerts one to a need for investigation.

A function of those with a gift for discerning spirits is to protect the innocent, the unwary, and even the foolish. All perpetrators and passive facilitators operate within these energy fields. Many, as we know, are attracted to Christian churches and hide within the church. Jennifer's step father was a model church member who regularly taught fifth and sixth grade boys at Sunday school. The BTK killer, Dennis Rader, was a faithful and involved member of his Lutheran Church and enjoyed such apparent standing that he was in a position of lay-leadership. Ted Bundy was vice-president of his Methodist Church council. Pedophile defrocked priest, John Geoghan, who became a symbol for the passive facilitator role played by a religious hierarchy, was murdered in prison by a fellow inmate. In all these, and the many similar cases, a satanically imbued energy field operates to protect the ongoing access to victims required by those who are ambulatory possessed or fatally possessed in order to act out the death-agenda.

Dennis Rader said, *"I just know it's a dark side of me. It kind of controls me. I personally think it's a – and I know it is not very Christian – but I actually think it's a demon that's within me. ...At some point and time it entered me when I was very young,"* said Rader.

In the words of Rader we see the crux of the problem. Jesus regularly cast out demons and modeled for us how to do the same. And yet, we have this profound disconnect rooted in a delusional energy field of selective blindness. It is no true Christianity that denies the existence of demons, that people can be oppressed, possessed, and controlled by satan and... that people can be powerfully and totally delivered by Jesus Christ. Rader, in a clever turn of phrase, invites us to agree that it's not Christian to think he could have a demon. In actuality we should expect that he does and act accordingly.

Preachers and priests, with few exceptions, are not speaking Biblical truth in regard to the occult. **Then the Lord said to me, "The prophets are prophesying falsehood in My name. I have neither sent them nor commanded them nor spoken to them; they are prophesying to you a false vision, divination, futility and deception of their own minds (Jeremiah 14: 14). Also Ezekiel 3: 17-19.**

One way that Tyler Deaton succeeded in operating his cult under the nose of International House of Prayer, using them, trading on their standing, is that when confronted or questioned he immediately adopted the appearance of being compliant and "teachable." It would have taken someone with a gift for discerning first the energy field, then the demonic attachments, to act on their gift by insisting the investigation go beyond the superficial. But, because these investigations are usually delegated to human resource departments or diplomatically gifted administrators who are invested in avoiding conflicts, the truth is derailed and a Biblical response is abandoned. Evil continues to operate to destructive outcomes. In this sad case it ended with the death of Bethany Ann Deaton. It is no coincidence that she was murdered on October 30th or that this cult was satanically assigned to International House of Prayer which, whether you agree with everything they espouse or not, does operate a 24 hour prayer ministry where many powerful intercessors are involved.

Some believers imagine that they can pray this gift into existence. It's attractive for all the wrong reasons. Nothing will circumvent and derail this gift more tragically than losing touch with the spiritual source from which this gift comes. ***Thus says the Lord God, "Woe to the foolish prophets who are following their own spirit and have seen nothing" (Ezekiel 13: 3).*** We might recall Jesus response to Peter. ***But turning around and seeing His disciples, He rebuked Peter and said, "Get behind Me, Satan; for you are not setting your mind on God's interests, but man's" (Mark 8: 33). Also Matthew 16: 23.***

Erecting these blindness-barriers is the work of unclean spirit beings and demons under satanic assignment and looking to partner with people and systems. Those that discern spirits will at times be that very unpopular figure that initiates the change that no one wants to see the need of. In recognizing human attachment with evil spirit beings and demons we are Holy Spirit informed about the cause and effect outcomes and can partner to avert consequences.

When I discern this disconnect, the erected and carefully maintained delusional barrier, I've learned to pay attention. Evil spirits recognize me as they do all Christians, all being Holy Spirit carriers. Present in circumstances and people, they give themselves away. ***And the evil spirit answered and said to them, "I recognize Jesus, and I know about Paul, but who are you? (Acts 19: 15).***

When the situational constructs of unseen spirits impact our awareness, we don't always have the language to interpret all the data we receive. What actually takes place when we discern spirits is far more than a feeling, though for lack of a better word "feeling" is the default word I try not to use.

The Jews asked how Jesus had become learned when no one had taught him. From a poor family of questionable birth, **nor appearance that we should be attracted to Him;** Jesus lacked the worldly credentials they respected. **So Jesus answered them and said, "My teaching is not Mine, but His who sent Me. If anyone is willing to do His will, he will know of the teaching, whether it is of God or whether I speak from Myself. He who speaks from himself seeks his own glory; but he who is seeking the glory of the One who sent Him, He is true, and there is no unrighteousness in Him (John 7: 16-18).**

For speaking thus the crowd said... **"You have a demon!"** Projection, scape-goating, and blame-shifting are common tools of demonically maneuvered humans. Stop being offended and shut down by such maneuvers. Paul encountered this same delusional blindness on a regular basis. **...just as it is written God gave them a spirit of stupor, eyes to see not and ears to hear not, down to this very day (Romans 11: 8).**

Another clue that satan is behind certain opposition is when worldly enemies that have hated one another and worked at cross purposes suddenly join forces. A macro example of this in coming prophecy will be when China and Russia attack Israel. A micro example: **And Herod with his soldiers, after treating Him with contempt and mocking Him, dressed Him in a gorgeous robe and sent Him back to Pilate. Now Herod and Pilate became friends with one another that very day; for before they had been enemies with each other (Luke 23: 11, 12).**

Isaiah wanted to know how long deluding spirits of blindness and deafness would frame the battle between good and evil. **Then I said, "Lord, how long?" And He answered. Until cities are devastated and without habitant, houses are without people and the land is utterly desolate (Isaiah 6: 11). Read Isaiah 6: 8-13.**

After an extended preternatural clash we may be weary and vulnerable to depression as Jonah was. Jesus alluded to the marvelous outcome of Jonah's ministry in eternal currency. **The men of Nineveh will stand up with this generation at the judgment, and will condemn it because they repented at the preaching of Jonah; and behold, something greater than Jonah is here (Matthew 12: 41).**

Blindness is the significant battle field encountered in the practice of deliverance. Not only does the person who clearly needs deliverance question the necessity as the time draws near, but those around them may do the same.

Today we would be wise to study the life and times of Christian martyr, Dietrich Bonheoffer. He not only opposed Nazism, but he opposed the amalgamized Christianity that bent to the will of Nazism and the political correctness of his day that rendered church leaders passive. Hitler used religious language. Many of the social elite, the intelligentsia, and the religious church celebrated this perfectly possessed vehicle of perdition as the savior of Germany. Bonheoffer, at age 27, gave one of the first speeches against the new chancellor, Adolf Hitler.

It is the role of faith to speak truth to morally bankrupt, lawless strongholds of power, greed, and lust. Doing so, may cost, but delayed will cost far more. Social action is a form of deliverance and a valid form of ministry. Paul told Timothy... ***O Timothy, guard what has been entrusted to you, avoiding worldly and empty chatter and the opposing arguments of what is falsely called "knowledge" which some have professed and thus gone astray from the faith. Grace be with you (1st Timothy 6: 20, 21).*** What are we up against? ***For this reason God will send upon them a deluding influence so that they will believe what is false, in order that they all may be judged who did not believe the truth, but took pleasure in wickedness (2nd Thessalonians 2: 11, 12).***

Expressing this evil dynamic in the context of law, Edmund Burke wrote of the Irish penal laws: *"A machine of wise and elaborate contrivance, as well fitted for the oppression, impoverishment and degradation of a people, and the debasement in them of human nature itself, as ever proceeded from the perverted ingenuity of man."*

Winston Churchill said: *"One ought never to turn ones back on a threatened danger and try to run away from it. If you do that, you will double the danger. But if you meet it promptly and without flinching, you will reduce the danger by half."*

And my favorite Winston quote for Christian's who won't risk conflict, won't recognize the battles and stick to the comfortably selected portions of scripture that feed their cowardice or excuse their greed: *"An appeaser is one who feeds the crocodile, hoping it will eat him last."*

Mordecai sent a reply to Esther that said in part. ***"And who knows whether you have not attained royalty for such a time as this?" (Esther 4: 14c).***

Paul instructed and then asserted the following. ***...but I want you to be wise in what is good and innocent in what is evil. The God of peace will soon crush Satan under your*** *feet. The grace of our Lord Jesus be with you (Romans 16: 19b, 20).*

Though His name has been hijacked throughout history God shows up for what He shows up for.

Now it came about when Joshua was by Jericho, that he lifted up his eyes and looked, and behold, a man was standing opposite him with his sword drawn in his hand, and Joshua went up to him and said to him, "Are you for us or for our adversaries?" He said, "No; rather I indeed come now as captain of the host of the Lord." And Joshua fell on his face to the earth, and bowed down, and said to him "What has my lord to say to his servant?" (Joshua 5: 13, 14.)

The horse is prepared for the day of battle, but the victory belongs to the Lord (Proverbs 21: 31).

CHAPTER NINE

MAJOR CORRECTIONS

Throughout history, man has experienced major threatening events and crisises that have afforded the faithful an opportunity to dislodge corrupt and toxic power strongholds. In these "corrections", the faithful have called out to God for justice. These cries do not fall on deaf ears. ***The Lord is not slow about His promise, as some count slowness, but is patient toward you, not wishing for any to perish but for all to come to repentance (2nd Peter 3: 9).***

The flood which saved mankind from coming extinction via assaults on the DNA of humans by the Nephilim is just one example from the pages of Scripture (Genesis 6 & 7). As a divine correction, whole civilizations have been wiped out: The Maya, who practiced human sacrifice despite an advanced scientific understanding of nature, astronomy, and the human body; Rome, once ruler of the known world, followed a similar trajectory; and the Nazi regime went the way of its blatantly satanic perpetrators. The fatally possessed Lenin and Stalin murdered more people within a geographical border than any antichrist of the last 200 years. ***The Son of God appeared for this purpose to destroy the works of the devil (1st John 3: 8b). (2nd Thessalonians 2: 8-12).***

Stemming such a crisis, while mitigating the consequences, true revival ushers in profound change and a return to the power and visionary constructs of a true faith. As believers we can usher in such a revival. It is absolutely within our authority as children of God to do so, and more and more saints have embraced this as a prayer calling.

Throughout Old Testament scripture we see that Father God postponed judgment when, the Hebrew people poured their repentant hearts out to Him. This could be the very reason why scripture tells us that only Father knows the date of the rapture, the start of Revelation events, and the return of Jesus Christ to planet earth in a final dramatic finish to recorded history as we know it. Perhaps, in God's very great mercy and divine-omnipotent status as Creator of all that has been created, this final judgment has already been postponed more than once because believers have interceded; prayed and fasted.

So many of us note the "birth pangs" and believe that God's return is eminent. I am waiting, I am watching. I pray that the flight of those living in Jerusalem will not be in winter nor on the Sabbath *(Matthew 24: 20)*. It pleases Him that together we are watching and reminding one another of the promise and splendor of His second coming. "Yes, come Lord, Jesus!" Marantha! *Revelation 19: 11-21.*

And on His robe and on His thigh He has a name written, "KING OF KINGS, AND LORD OF LORDS (Revelation 19: 16). Right now a revolution of revival is needed in the church, and my prayer is that it will happen very soon.

When the Hebrew priesthood failed in the appointed role that God designed them to embrace and practice, the culture was very quickly impacted. This failure of spiritual leadership and adherence to God's word as written go hand in hand. As pagan influence infiltrates the religious systems, tolerance for sin opens doors that usher in political and societal corruption at ever growing levels of toxicity.

The church is meant to be the powerful front line offensive. If a church denies the supernatural power of being alive in faith, failing to engage they look more and more like the world. They become complacent and blind to the salt-less path to which they have corporately turned their course.

One role of the church *...and to bring to light what is the administration of the mystery which for ages has been hidden in God who created all things; so that the manifold wisdom of God might now be made known through the church to the rulers and authorities in the heavenly places (Ephesians 3: 9, 10).*

It's called warfare for a reason. After praying and fasting Daniel was visited by an angel who explained why the answer was delayed. Intercessory prayer, as a matter of warfare, is the prescriptive antidote. *But the prince of the kingdom of Persia was withstanding me for twenty one days; then behold, Michael, one of the chief princes, came to help me, for I had been left there with the kings of Persia (Daniel 10: 13). Hebrews 1: 14*

All of us experience what we consider delay in seeing answers to our prayers. As quoted earlier, God isn't slow about his promises, but here we may be experiencing delay as opposition. Try to see it... an entirely different oppositional dynamic, a cornered territorial spirit and his demon-minions holding back those angels of God in the spirit realm. Choose your words like sprays of bullets; quote scripture in the authority of one covered by the blood of Jesus Christ. Pray with fervent and deliberate intention that as angel-messengers, ministering-angels, and angel-warriors fly into battle, for that purpose to which you've committed the words of your heart and God has committed His troops, opposition will be utterly and completely swept away by the fire of the Holy Spirit.

When a major correction looms, most often by the third generation, what has passed for legitimate faith is now dull and tarnished. Those benefiting are invested in preternatural blindness and fiercely opposed to change. This is where we are today, at the end of a cyclical process in tolerance to sin and with a major correction just around the bend.

Significant stays of the judgment that threatens a nation and a people, begin when the Holy Spirit convicts and opens the eyes of the heart to feel grief. ***The Lord replied, "If you return to me I will restore you so you can continue to serve Me. If you speak words that are worthy you will be my spokesman. You are to influence them; do not let them influence you! (Jeremiah 15 19)***

When a revival-restoration is pervasive and genuine the Holy Spirit reveals Himself in miracles, healing, and powerful manifestations of grace. Major corrections of judgment are averted. This may begin with a small group of believers praying and fasting. Revival is accompanied by disclosure and repentance; the precursor to healing. The strength of any revival is seen in the fruit of change that follows. No lasting change – no fruit – equals false revival.

And if you extract the precious from the worthless, you will become My spokesman. They for their part may turn to you, but as for you, you must not turn to them (Jeremiah 15: 19b) NAS

Expect warfare if you are praying for revival, moving beyond passivity and the lie that change is not possible. Across denominational divides, across this world, many have set themselves apart for this purpose, standing as a fortified wall. ***"Then I will make you to this people a fortified wall of bronze; and though they fight against you, they will not prevail over you; for I am with you to save you and deliver you," declares the Lord (Jeremiah 15: 20).***

In our changed way of looking at spiritual warfare and understanding how the immaterial impacts the material, we realize that our impacting the culture for Christ is not a passive enterprise. With the ever more sensitive "eyes of our heart" we are equipped to oppose the imprints, the infestations, and the influence.

Paul is transparent in reminding us of his former status as an enemy of God. He says: ***I did it in ignorance and unbelief.*** Paul put many of the early Christians in jail. ***I hunted down His people, harming them in every way I could.*** Nevertheless

God saved this sinner. Paul said: *How thankful I am to Christ Jesus our Lord for considering me trustworthy and appointing me to serve Him.*

As a Christian you are likewise called to a special appointment, and in the authority and gifting of this appointment you have everything you need in Christ to be successful. *...seeing that His divine power has granted to us everything pertaining to life and godliness, through the true knowledge of Him who called us by His own glory and excellence (2nd Peter 1: 3).*

This is a true saying, and everyone should believe it: Christ, Jesus came into the world to save sinners-and I was the worst of them (1st Timothy 1: 15). Excerpts from 1st Timothy 1: 12-20.

There is only one answer for an epoch of time that is careening toward judgment. The modern church must reject the pharisaical "religious" curse of merging faith with culture. We cannot manufacture the kind of grief and remorse that brings personal forgiveness and significant micro and/or, macro revival. No slick preaching or bullying style of rebuttal penetrates the unwilling heart.

Even to wayward believers, our loving Savior remains ever present and accessible. *If we are faithless, He remains faithful, for He cannot deny Himself (2nd Timothy 2: 13).* It is never too late to do an about face.

Only after the prophet Nathan had pointed his sin out to him, did David become honest, shattering the delusional façade of sufficiency. As this process began the Holy Spirit stripped away layers of self-centered blindness which actively partnered to build a stronghold of preternatural captivity. As the scales were stripped from his eyes, David shared the solution, writing Psalm 51. *Wash me thoroughly from my iniquity and cleanse me from my sin. For I know my transgressions, and my sin is ever before me (Psalm 51: 2, 3).*

The significant phrase is, *"For I know my transgressions."* When such painful willingness to face the truth is embraced judgment is averted.

If I shut up the heavens so that there is no rain, or if I command the locust to devour the land, or if I spread pestilence among My people, and My people who are called by My name humble themselves and pray and seek My face and turn from their wicked ways, then I will hear from heaven, will forgive their sin and will heal their land (2nd Chronicles 7: 13, 14).

Intercessory prayer and corporate deliverance open the doors to revival and reformation. *Truly I say to you, whatever you bind on earth shall have been bound in heaven; and whatever you loose on earth shall be loosed in heaven (Matthew 18: 18).*

I will give you the keys to the kingdom of heaven; and whatever you bind on earth shall have been bound in heaven, and whatever you loose on earth shall have been loosed in heaven (Matthew 16: 19).

As you move toward that place where you pray, imagine the literal keys to the kingdom of heaven in the palm of your hand. There isn't one key, but many. Oh, Lord, which keys to use today?

Do you see it? As a son or daughter of the Most High King you are invited to embrace the very inheritance afforded by salvation. Among all the riches God has provided, you additionally own this precious and powerful set of keys. The words of your prayers open and close doors. In concert with God revealing His will to you, you send out troops of warring and ministering angels. By grace the keys to the kingdom of God turn effortlessly in the lock. By grace there is no rust to slow you down. Furthermore the key you select swings the door wide on its hinges so that you can step into His awesome, receptive presence. It is to this place that we, as Holy Spirit carriers sealed by grace, are drawn time and time again. Repentance makes this possible. Openness to believe and receive His word empowers you. Intercessory prayer transports you.

Now, as you step across the threshold, *"you have come to Mount Zion and the city of the living God, the heavenly Jerusalem, and to myriads of angels" (Hebrews 12: 22).* Covered by His blood, in covenant and intimacy, you pour your heart out to Jesus Christ. You tell Him what you need and what you desire. There are great burdens that may seem impossible to humanly fix. By contrast, other burdens may seem incidental, but are heard by no less a receptive ear. *...whatever you bind on earth shall have been bound in heaven; and whatever you loose on earth shall be loosed in heaven. AMEN!*

What I've found about prayer is that God changes my heart. I begin praying one way, telling Jesus what I think and what I want Him to do for me and even foolishly, how to do it and when. Then, miracle of miracles, Jesus realigns my focus and draws me to pray in a different way. Sometimes an entirely different way.

And He Himself bore our sins in His body on the cross, so that we might die to sin and live to righteousness; for by His wounds you were healed. For you were continually straying like sheep, but now you have returned to the Shepherd and Guardian of your souls (1st Peter 2: 24, 25).

What is wrong with many current church structures in the self-sufficient pockets of the world that preclude them from being the catalyst in a collective ground swell of salt and light revival? The visionary gifts and acts-model of church governance is largely absent.

Today, most pastors are primarily shepherds, teachers, or evangelists and the preaching style of a pastor reflects a calling in one of these three pastor areas. A pastor who is a prophet-evangelist sees the big picture. They want to get people saved and are then ready to move on. They will never be the shepherd who spends hours hearing the details of personal problems and yet, if they are a single pastor in a church, the uninformed church body will very likely have unreasonable expectations. It's not that the prophet-evangelist lacks empathy. They have compassion for numbers of people coming to Christ and were not designed to operate as long term mentors.

Others are needed to pick up the teaching and shepherding responsibilities of pastors whose principal calling is to be an Evangelist. Whether a mega church, a home church, or a store front startup church, the early model was for lay persons to become part of the fabric of church life. In this way people learned how to walk out the blessing of a dynamic calling.

But you are a chosen race, a royal priesthood, a Holy nation, a people for God's own possession, so that you may proclaim the excellencies of Him who called you out of darkness into His marvelous light, for you once were not a people, but now you are the people of God; you had not received mercy, but now you have received mercy (1st Peter 2: 9, 10).

A pastor who is a counselor-shepherd may have trouble saying no and can initially lack boundaries, learning through experience how to function in a way that allows time for rest and family. These pastors have a powerful gift of mercy and are able to evidence the love of Christ, which very much enriches any congregation. Shepherds are popular with staff and are far more comfortable working where God designed them to serve in areas of mentoring, teaching, and healing. In this pursuit, without a strong administrator working alongside them, other important areas can fail by default.

Pastor-teachers will usually pass out a sermon outline. They want people to know what they believe and why; a really good thing in this day and age when one can sit through an entire sermon and hear very little of the Word of God. After I first came to faith in Jesus Christ God placed me in such a congregation with a pastor I'll always be grateful to, Pastor Ed Davis. This is just where I needed to be, soaking up the fundamentals of a solid Biblical understanding. After I was particularly wounded in a long assault that lasted three years God placed me in a small church with Pastor Arnold Roberts. Arnold has a strong shepherding gift with a healing and miracles kind of faith. Again, God was so good, having me land where healing was abundant.

If pastors and priests who are also teachers are strong in a hands-on gifting of leadership and administration, they may leave little room for the Holy Spirit to operate. They are often accused of being too corporate and might counter this by pointing out all that is materially being accomplished. They desperately need the balance provided by those that are gifted in other areas.

A pastor who has been personally hurt will sometimes not trust involving others in service. It will be hard for them to share responsibility. These are the churches that fail to mature and risk. Saints that spiritually mature beyond a certain point leave these churches. They are Holy Spirit compelled to be involved in ministry and seek a greater connectedness in order to do so.

Do we get the picture? No pastor or priest was designed to act alone attempting the impossible task of being all things to all people. If placed on a pedestal and isolating themselves from valid censure they will certainly fail. Not only do many congregations have wrong expectations of those in full time service, but many in service have been let down by both their training and church leadership.

Too much unhealthy control, and too few boundaries with little control... these are different problems with one foundational solution; a person with an anointing to lead as an apostle. Apostle is both an office and a confluence of spiritual gifts which characterizes a specific calling. People and churches that deny that miracles and healing happen today are required to say that the spiritual gift of apostle fell out of use after Pentecost, or with the death of John, the last of the original apostles and the only one to die of old age. This is an untenable position since Paul called himself an apostle and apostle is listed among the gifts.

It's important to note that this confusion falls in line with the satanic agenda to strip visionary gifts from use in the church. *The signs of a true apostle were performed among you with all perseverance, by signs and wonders and miracles (2nd Corinthians 12: 12).*

An apostle is someone who makes room for visionary gifts operating in the body of Christ to which he is responsible for overseeing. The verse isn't saying that a person with an apostle gift has all these gifts, but he does facilitate them and would have a strong gift of discerning spirits. A genuine faith in the context of apostle is attested to by signs and wonders and miracles occurring under such leadership. Not vested with a single person, but through a confluence of gifts operating through all believers.

The personal visionary experience ushers in a radical paradigm shift. Read **2ⁿᵈ Corinthians 12: 1-6**. Note the humble way that Paul conveys this experience. After Peter and John healed the lame beggar they were put in jail. **Read Acts chapters 3 and 4.**

On the next day they were then brought before Annas the high priest *and all who were of priestly descent.* Realizing that they could not explain the miracle away, nor were they ever going to contain the Christ/Messiah-word from spreading, they demanded that Peter and John... *not to speak or teach at all in the name of Jesus. But Peter and John answered and said to them, "Whether it is right in the sight of God to give heed to you rather than to God, you be the judge; for we cannot stop speaking about what we have seen and heard" (Acts 4: 18b-20). .*

Those who are apostles are compelled to revive and transform unhealthy structures and will speak truth to the infestation within toxic strongholds. We all need accountability and those gifted with apostle leadership are no exception. It isn't my intention here to write in depth about the office of apostle. It does however need to be mentioned because where this office is lacking, denied, or denigrated the visionary gifts lose their God-ordered place.

A very serious sin is the casual way that the Lord's Supper is taken and viewed. Consider and ponder how communion is conducted in your church. Is there a genuine call to repentance? Is there a reverent understanding of what communion is and represents?

Therefore, whoever eats the bread or drinks the cup of the Lord in an unworthy manner; shall be guilty of the body and the blood of the Lord. But a man must examine himself, and in so doing he is to eat of the bread and drink of the cup. For he who eats and drinks, eats and drinks judgment to himself if he does not judge the body rightly. For this reason many among you are weak and sick and a number sleep (1ˢᵗ Corinthians 11: 27-30.)

The five primary sins of the religious church that stand in satanic opposition to blessing, restoration, and revival are:
- Lack of reverence for the Lord's Supper.
- Lack of apostle leadership and refusal to accept such leadership.
- Failure to institute church discipline.
- Failure to teach and preach against pagan occult constructs.

- Failure to offer restoration with aftercare through deliverance, exorcism, and healing.

Paul expressed his calling as being real in that the outcome of his ministry was the irrefutable evidence of God setting him apart, sealing him to fulfill the office of apostle. *Am I not free? Am I not an apostle? Have I not seen Jesus our Lord? If to others I am not an apostle, at least I am to you; for you are the seal of my apostleship in the Lord (1st Corinthians 9: 1, 2).*

Paul felt the need to defend his authority and calling. When church leaders with an apostle calling arrive on the scene, they tend to encounter preternatural opposition. They are interested in the body of Christ, having the willingness to be real, the integrity to be faithful, and the courage to be honest. Apostles are likely to invite those who criticize and sinfully gossip to change their behavior or leave the church. They will say to those who have held the purse strings and constrained ministry that gifts of stewardship and discernment will operate in the area of giving. Sometimes they survive a new appointment and the body of Christ matures and thrives; too often they are labeled troublemakers and end up leaving their denominations.

And He gave some as apostles, and some as prophets, and some as evangelists, and some as pastors and teachers, for the equipping of the saints for the work of service, to the building up of the body of Christ; until we all attain to the unity of the faith, and of the knowledge of the Son of God, to a mature man, to the measure of the stature which belongs to the fullness of Christ (Ephesians 4: 11-13). Also 1st Corinthians 12: 27, 28.

So ask yourself? Why would "apostle" be included in this New Testament list if all these were not also current spiritual gifts intended to be fully operational today? And why did Paul vehemently defend his apostle calling if not for those who came after him in subsequent generations?

Although they would not agree and would blindly defend their position, all unhealthy churches, on some level, evidence the manipulative self-centered viewpoint that the word of God and rules don't apply to them. It becomes necessary to fit Biblical constructs to traditions and denominational bias and format. *For the time will come when they will not endure sound doctrine, but wanting to have their ears tickled, they will accumulate for themselves teachers in accordance to their own desires and will turn away their ears from the truth and will turn aside to myths (2nd Timothy 4: 3, 4).*

91

Structures can take on narcissistic characteristics. It is in these churches that we see extremes of legalism or, conversely, the loss of identity. With the loss of identity, churches are satanically charged with fitting in, serving the societal and cultural norms. Over the last decades we've seen these denominational hierarchies battle with their local churches. We've seen other denominations foster a bunker mentality to isolate and self-protect. Each represents an extreme stance outside the will of God.

That the religious church today has little real authority is informed by the description and overview of the seven churches in Revelation, chapters two and three. Laodicea is the place no church or church leader, in whatever age, wants to be: Tolerating sin, taking a passive stance, and being the passive facilitator during an epoch of history when evil floods the breach. *I know your deeds, that you are neither cold nor hot, I wish that you were cold or hot. So because you are lukewarm, and neither hot nor cold, I will spit you out of My mouth (Revelation 3: 15, 16).* **Church of Laodicea, Rev: 3: 14-22**

Many American churches today would not risk saying with the apostle Paul, *I turned them over to Satan so they would learn not to blaspheme God (1st Timothy 1: 20b).* **1st Corinthians 5: 3-5**

Let's give an example. In the church is a couple. The wife is addicted to gambling and impoverishes her family. The pastor is confused about why the family is dependent on the church to provide money for utilities and gifts for Christmas. Finally the truth is known.

In another example a man who tithes regularly is abusive to his wife. Sometimes his children appear with bruises and the pastor is notified. The church reports what they suspect, but little more is done. To interfere is seen as too assertive a response implying judgment.

Over time, the pattern of practice continues in both families. Both unabashedly remain in church. The pastor realizes that this allows the two perpetrators to conceal who they are while continuing to manipulate the enabling spouses. The church is tolerating and partnering with sin.

What to do? Lifted as a principal from scripture the answer is, "tough love." *Do you not know that a little leaven leavens the whole lump of dough? Clean out the old leaven so that you may be a new lump, just as you are in fact unleavened. For Christ our Passover also has been sacrificed. Therefore let us celebrate the feast, not with old leaven, nor with the leaven of malice and wickedness, but with the unleavened bread of sincerity and truth (1st*

Corinthians 5: 6b-8).

Judgment - Just saying the word today causes some to immediately bristle in offense. How dare we judge? They have been indoctrinated to the out of context, politically correct construct that Christians are judgmental and on the defensive and must therefore prove to the world that they are not. The next time you hear this, please speak up; correct this lie of satan. God gave us facilities of discernment to examine and weigh the consequences of sin in ourselves, in others, and in our world. We do so out of moral responsibility. However, in the context of faith we do not judge outsiders. Again, because according to the word of God they are already under divine judgment and need the love of Jesus Christ.

If you read 1st Corinthians 5 in context, Paul makes clear that we had better be judging one another and holding ourselves and other believers who may have lost perspective or be too weak or blinded by circumstances that they've forgotten Biblical truth and lost their way. Bringing a brother or sister back to the fullness of faith in Christ causes joyful celebration in heaven. Jesus said: *In the same way, I tell you, there is joy in the presence of the angels of God over one sinner who repents (Luke 15: 10).*

For those believers who will not listen to reproof or be restored; preferring sin, God says to remove them from the church. *For what have I to do with judging outsiders? Do you not judge those who are within the church? But those who are outside, God judges. Remove the wicked man from among yourselves (1st Corinthians 5: 12). Also James 4: 17.*

A common refrain in AA and Al-anon is, "you are as sick as your secrets." The most telling barometer of a church or Christian ministry can be seen in how they manage scandal. When I'm called to deliverance I want to know "What don't I know." I may discern a dysfunctional stronghold, but I don't yet have full disclosure.

When scandals arise, it's important to evaluate the response. Has the truth been hidden? Were best practices followed? If children were hurt or if a significant theft has taken place were the authorities notified? Or did someone decide this wasn't necessary calling instead a public relations firm to reframe the information that gets out? Did a few people hide information from the membership or pretend the crime or scandal didn't happen. Or worse still, did the leadership minimize their role in failing to act in the early stages. Did they decide to self-protect, avoiding personal censure via the rationalization that disclosure would hurt the kingdom of God.

Organizations that react in this way have not made room for the visionary gifts, nor do they have apostle leadership. At such a time, there is no prophet to show up and point out how such a cowardly reaction displeases the Lord Jesus Christ. There is no saint with the gift of discerning spirits to recognize the preternatural imprints. There is no shepherd-healer who sees the crisis as an opportunity to heal the wounds that have gone unrecognized. Nor is there an intercessor-evangelist to turn the hearts of the people toward repentant prayer and fasting.

Saints with these spiritual gifts are somewhere close, but they have been denied a role. The gifts they have are a threat to the status quo, have not been nurtured and empowered. Failing to be recognized, they would not be invited into the solution; both a tragedy and a fatal flaw of leadership.

Dishonest solutions always impact subsequent generations of pastors and church members. Preternatural blindness sets in. Justifying the bad decisions will take precedence. Protecting the sin will become strategy, and then policy. Before we know it, deliverance from evil spirits is needed in--of all places--the church. Why? Because no matter how many people are sitting in the pews every Sunday, this church or organization has handed over legal access to the enemy.

Before Me there was no God formed, and there will be none after Me. I, even I, am the Lord, and there is no savior besides Me. It is I who have declared and saved and proclaimed, and there was no strange god among you; so you are My witnesses," declares the Lord, "And I am God. Even from eternity I am He, and there is none who can deliver out of My hand; I act and who can reverse it?" (Isaiah 43: 10c-13). Apostles are designed to confront sin head-on in order to keep ministry alive and healthy.

I've seen much abuse associated with tongues and especially in regard to the visionary gifts. Tongues must not be contrived or practiced until one gets the syntax and rhythm down. Tongues come from the Holy Spirit. Posturing tongues puts this practice on an occult level with mindless chanting, and can give legal access to a demon spirit since, in this case, tongues is not from God.

Not every person who speaks in tongues has a visionary gift. Not every person who has a visionary gift speaks in tongues. Tongues is a supernatural manifestation of God moving through us; an expression of the Holy Spirit.

In a Bible study I taught I became friends with a woman who belonged to a thriving church. As I got to know her I was surprised at how little of scripture she actually knew. She told me her pastor didn't approve of her attending our neighborhood Bible study because it wasn't "sanctioned." To get it sanctioned, she invited me to visit her church.

94

We first attended what was called Sunday school. Led by a music-leader and a "teacher", there was no reciprocal exchange taking place. There were also no Bibles, not even for visitors. Most everyone spoke in tongues. No one interpreted, and if you were not standing in the aisle, you were rocking back and forth in your seat with your arms wrapped about your body. The music was so loud that I worried for the ears of the infants sitting on their mother's laps.

This single Sunday school class, devoid of teaching, ended. No one left the sanctuary. More people filtered in and soon the actual service began. The pastor's sermon was peppered by more people spontaneously speaking in tongues and no attempt to interpret so that others could benefit. What I saw was a commitment to self-serving emotionalism which, as an outlet, can be as addictive and opens the door to demonic access. I was reminded of the contrast between pagan worship and Isaiah's prophetic delivery of the inspired word of God as recounted in *1st Kings 18: 20-40*. To understand these vivid contrasts study this chapter. Isaiah prayed: *Answer me, O Lord, answer me that this people may know that You, O Lord, are God, and that You have turned their heart back again (1st Kings 18: 37).*

By contrast I attended a summer prayer group at a First Assembly of God Church. Some spoke in tongues as they prayed. I didn't know what was actually said and another woman didn't always interpret, but my spirit sang with what the Holy Spirit was expressing in a heavenly language.

On another occasion I attended a highly charged service in which the screaming pastor had most of his congregation cowering in their seats. During a prior service, when it was time for the offering, this same pastor suggested that all the women put their wedding rings in the basket. A couple of hours later, in the midst of lunch, the first phone calls came in requesting the jewelry back. This little incident made the local news and was a black eye to the body of Christ.

We love to be amused at the Mr. Collins character in Pride and Prejudice. It's about to storm, but he keeps his rural parishioners captive as he drones on and on. Collins is one of many narcissistic personalities from literature. He just happens to also be a narcissist who has a church appointment.

With my friend, Nina, I traveled to hear a well-known Christian speaker in a neighboring state. When it was time for the offering, the person officiating made the statement that he would never say that deliverance could be had by the making of a financial gift. He then made himself out to be a liar. Nina and I looked at each other in disgust as he proclaimed that a generous monetary gift could guarantee deliverance during the prayer time that followed.

Another sadly memorable incident occurred in a gathering of staff members in a mainstream denominational church. The woman pastor suggested that we all line up and march around the church in celebration of women. She passed around a copy of the "chant" we were to recite. Not one mention of Jesus, but a telling reference to the goddess. I was opening my mouth when another believer assumed the honor of denouncing such a travesty and affront to Jesus Christ.

I've heard many false beliefs expressed by Christian people and I've held some myself. I wrote a book some years ago that is off the market and in it I expressed some of what I was taught that in practice the Holy Spirit revealed as wrong. One, that Christian people cannot have a demon. Christians can have a demonic infestation that sets up in the flesh. Their homes can be haunted and they can be horribly and fatally addicted.

Another falsehood I had to repent of, since I taught it, is that all ghosts are demons impersonating dead people. Some are, but there are various other kinds of evil spirits that have rebelled against God's kingdom, authority, and rule.

If the Holy Spirit draws one to give up a lie, we are wise to do so. As comforter, He'll replace that false belief with riches that heal. Pray, "Lord Jesus, please deliver me from deception, illusion, delusion, and incorrect beliefs." Read His word. What you need is there, ready, welcoming, and life changing. *All Scripture is inspired by God and profitable for teaching, for reproof, for correction, for training in righteousness; so that the man of God may be adequate, for every good work (2nd Timothy 3: 16, 17).*

Giving up a lie means that we must admit that we are wrong. I've personally had a lot of lies I needed to let go of; even repent of. Some of these lies I absorbed via religious tradition. Some were inherited inclinations and predispositions rooted in past generational sin. Other deceptions I was taught, while the majority came at first unconsciously from deeply embedded fears and trauma. I needed both counseling and deliverance. Don't ever be afraid to ask God to reveal the truth about what you believe and then unashamedly proclaim His goodness for doing so. Our strength comes from being authentic.

Do not quench the Spirit; do not despise prophetic utterances. But examine everything carefully; hold fast to what is good; abstain from every form of evil (1st Thessalonians 5: 19-22).

Finally there is no perfect church on earth. My work has taken me into many. On two occasions I performed a deliverance of place in churches where demonic infestations were harming ministry and causing dissention. Bill Bean has had the same experience of being called to a church for a similar purpose.

If you're waiting for perfection you won't find it. Sharpen your discernment gifts and go to church. Whether your gift is fully understood or appreciated is not the point. Obedience is the point. Offer and make known your spiritual gift of discerning spirits. You are to influence them. They are not to influence you.

Every person with this gift of discerning spirits is called to the fray; not the sidelines. You are a bond-servant of Christ. This means we lay aside ambivalence and work within His design for us; placing ourselves under His authority and will.

Little children, let us not love with word or with tongue, but in deed and truth (1st John 3: 18).

CHAPTER TEN

NARCISSISTIC PERSONALITY DISORDER and THE ALLIGATOR FARM

Preternatural energy fields of blindness are most clearly discerned around those that exhibit, Narcissistic Personality Disorder. Just as demonic infestations are established in certain regions and places they are also grouped in and around certain people. God has given some believers a kind of radar to discern these human spirits long before behavior exposes those under such satanic control. Some of these damaged people hide in the religious, out of balance church which affords them a narcissistic supply of victims and additionally provides the veneer of respectability.

Narcissistic people cannot sustain reciprocal relationships. Religious scripts and language with no real depth attract these people. Any lasting relationships are dependent and enmeshed alliances where a passive-facilitator-partner has been systematically groomed to abdicate responsibility; reflecting the ego and doing the will of the perpetrator/narcissist.

These lost people tend to have a story which they stick to, refine, and obsess over as a kind of identity; a living thing over which they attempt to exercise absolute control; not realizing the degree to which they are controlled by evil. Confront the facts or introduce another point of view and you are immediately identified as an enemy. There is a carefully constructed rendition of the story fitted to almost any given situation over which they have human authority. Out of this the preternatural imprint works and seeks to train those brought under this sphere of influence on how to think and feel. The goal is to disable critical thinking skills. Do we see the value of various spiritual gift-sets working through the grace of God—reading the subtext, counting the fruit, discerning the spirits and taking a stand?

These people need our prayers and compassion, even when we've legitimately decided they are not safe to be around. A miracle is needed by way of a supernatural deliverance. For purposes of deliverance we see this as a satanic area of bondage and stronghold of denial of the truth of one's sinful state apart from Jesus Christ. Separation from the delusional stronghold is a life and death struggle.

Some are attracted to busy churches or to the salt-less institutional church. Conscious or not, they are sent under specific satanic assignment. They may appear to make excellent members, tithe regularly, and volunteer for lay positions of authority. Here they would be serving their father satan, restraining and controlling ministry as far as reach is allowed to extend.

In the next chapter we'll look at some characters from film, including Violet from the movie, *Suddenly Last Summer*. Reading her behavior we will consider the extremes this narcissistic mother went to in order to preserve her story as a reflection of identity and a living testament to her dead son – the narcissistic supply.

I don't know who coined the phrase, narcissistic supply, but it aptly describes the unreasonable need for these people to have, at all times a ready supply of victims whose job it is to mirror how they see themselves. Having no awareness of who they really are, how wretched and sinful, they find their identity in the ways they manipulate others to buy into the worship of self. Many demons work through these people. With preternatural assistance and direction they act out the infantile demand to have all their emotional and physical needs met by dominating the will and focusing the resources of those around them on themselves. Depending on the level of intelligence and social sophistication they can be quite devious and subtle.

Satan uses these people to waste time and resources. Their interactions have the potential to be personally assaultive to others and especially when given access to weaker or younger persons. Believers with the spiritual gift of discerning spirits can work with these people; though we usually start out angering them as we interject the truths of scripture and confront the walls of self-deception. Expect them to turn on you. Why? We are not buying the alligator farm otherwise known as the story behind which evil hides, concealing the imprint, the infestation, and the influence.

As leaders these people carefully select beholden or morally vulnerable individuals to partner with. In the work place they are hyper sensitive to criticism and if allowed, will fire those who object to their tactics rather than work with them.

Narcissists are prime candidates for demonic control since they are essentially empty. They receive preternaturally exchanged information and direction that allow them to operate undetected, sometimes for a lifetime. Much energy and resources are spent on maintaining a respectable façade. Most never break the law and so must be recognized for the subtle ways they invade boundaries and commit moral assaults. The last thing a possessing demon wants is to give up its human conduit, especially if that human conduit is an essentially empty narcissist.

Psychiatrist, M. Scott Peck has passed on to glory, but provides the best succinct, clinical summary of core traits which evil people evidence as patterns of practice that I have read. He challenged his peers to consider that evil should be a psychological, spiritual, and medical diagnostic category; a novel idea when the book first came out. Speaking in the confluence of medicine and faith, Peck makes the point that evil people evidence the following narcissistic behaviors. Quote below from: *People of the Lie: The hope for healing human evil; M. Scott Peck; Simon and Schuster; Copyright: Library of Congress; ISBN: 0-684-84859-7*

- **Consistent destructive, scapegoating behavior, which may often be quite subtle.**
- **Excessive, albeit usually covert, intolerance to criticism and other forms of narcissistic injury.**
- **Pronounced concern with a public image and self image of respectability, contributing to a stability of lifestyle but also to pretentiousness and denial of hateful feelings or vengeful motives.**
- **Intellectual deviousness, with an increased likelihood of a mild schizophrenic like disturbance of thinking at times of stress.**

What I like about how Peck has framed these traits, evidenced in behavior as a consistent strategy for navigating conflict, is that seen as a whole they provide a context for us to implement a valuable assessment tool in the practice of deliverance.

In one situation I was asked to pray deliverance for a family that had a narcissistic adult daughter. The diagnosis was made by a treating psychiatrist while the parents still had the authority to insist on treatment. Years later, shaken by a recent incident, they wanted to know if she was also demon possessed. I'll call her Sandi. Sandi had done so much damage to her parents and siblings that they were afraid of her. One brother had a restraining order against her. At one point her parents filed charges and she spent time in jail. This woman who, at first meeting, was quite lovely and articulate saw things very differently from her victims. She blamed her family for all her problems and saw herself as the primary victim.

At first she relished the attention. As we talked she seemed to operate with few internal filters. This abruptly changed as she realized I wasn't "buying the alligator farm."

Family structures with one parent evidencing narcissistic behavior and the other parent playing the role of the passive facilitator creates a toxic milieu dangerous to children. In these circumstances one child can be singled out to play the role of the

101

scapegoat. This is usually a child that calls attention to the unhealthy family dynamics by rebelling or attempting suicide or overcoming the intimidation scripts by reporting the abuse. While it may not seem so, they are usually the healthier sibling. In these family structures, it is the cruelly assigned job of this proxy-scapegoat-child to deflect attention away from the perpetrator-narcissist. There is a story to tell about how bad the scapegoat is and too often, poorly trained social workers, with no discernment skills, buy the story. This deflects attention from the hyper sensitive, sometimes psychopathic perpetrator-parent.

These children grow up to be hurting adults in need of healing and validation for what they've been through. Often time they don't feel free to acknowledge what they've suffered. It was never safe to be truly genuine; just to be who God created them to be. Sadly in marriage many choose partners that will never love them. There is much unhealed trauma and many false scripts which prevent them from trusting the love of God. All this can be broken in deliverance.

In Sandi's case she had never been the family scapegoat. It was important for me to evaluate this; depending on Jesus Christ to reveal truth. It's import to ask God... is there something more you are showing me that I'm not seeing?

Prolonged exposure to the narcissist means that by transference demons camp on the legalistic satanic principal that they've been given legal access to generationally harm other family members. I prayed for Sandi's healing and was able to talk with her on more than one occasion, but other than to manipulate me into reframing her family's conception of her so that she could regain access to the narcissistic supply, and especially her nieces and nephews, she wasn't interested in a miracle of God via a supernatural deliverance, separating her from the demons she willingly partnered with.

A childhood biking accident and head injury was cited as the possible turning point in the personality changes that culminated in Sandi's psychopathic, narcissistic behavior. What comes first; the chicken or the egg? I don't know. Some that have no apparent contributing history of trauma or brain injury may choose the evil path via small measured steps. Some may have a contributing history of profound trauma; emotional or physical abuse. Patterns of behavior change brain chemistry. Where demons are operational in flesh a profound injury exists to which Jesus consistently evidences tremendous mercy. When asked for healing His response was in the affirmative. ***Jesus stretched out His hand and touched him, saying, "I am willing, be cleansed (Matthew 8: 3). Jesus said to him, "I will come and heal him (Matthew 8: 7).***

There is only one path to healing in deliverance from evil spirits and that is through Jesus Christ (***Romans 10: 9, 10***). There are times when we must separate from dangerous people no matter how connected they may be to our life history. We turn this person over to consequences so that God can work in their lives, but also to self-protect ourselves and others; not being part of the problem. ***So then it does not depend on the man who wills or the man who runs, but on God who has mercy (Romans 9: 16).*** We let go and let God.

When I asked if I could pray for Sandi, she declined. When I asked if she thought she was demonically controlled as her parents believed, she got up and left the room. But not before we exchanged a look that sent an electric charge of offense and recognition through my body as it always does. I had seen "it" and "it" had looked back at me. I told Sandi that she should imagine the door to healing in Jesus Christ as always being open.

Jesus summoned His twelve disciples and gave them authority over unclean spirits to cast them out, and to heal every kind of disease and every kind of sickness (Matthew 10: 1). Matthew 18: 19, 20, Luke 10: 19, 20, Mark 16: 17, 18.

When evening came, after the sun had set, they began bringing to Him all who were ill and those who were demon possessed. And the whole city had gathered at the door. And He healed many who were ill with various diseases; and He was not permitting the demons to speak, because they knew who He was (Mark 1: 32-34). John 14: 11-15

As Christians we believe in radical change. We hold out hope that any can be saved and we avoid word curses that say otherwise. An example of such a radical core-healing is, of course, the apostle Paul. Another comes from the life of the last king of Judah. ***(2nd Kings 21: 1-8).*** Manasseh was raised with every advantage. He followed his God-fearing father, Hezekiah, to the throne, but is revealed as the worst possible sinner.

For he built altars for all the host of heaven in the two courts of the house of the Lord. He made his son pass through the fire, practiced witchcraft and used divination, and dealt with mediums and spiritists. He did much evil in the sight of the Lord provoking Him to anger (2nd Kings 21: 4-6).

To understand how evil this leader was, the degree to which he had invited the demonic to rule his life, allowing and sweeping in devastating consequences which tore apart a country and a people, it would be necessary to read ***2nd Kings 21.*** We have many antichrist examples from history. The resultant atrocities' challenge

103

us to never passively accept such burgeoning usurpation of power. Not in our homes, our communities, our country, nor the world. A sovereign God has equipped us to recognize evil; to unmask such evil. For all intents and purposes Manasseh was a practicing satanist who carried out human sacrifice, including his own son burned alive in the fire in homage to a devil. He worshipped multiple pagan gods, and defiled the temple.

Those who have the visionary gift of discerning spirits would have a strong sense of the partnerships in place between Manasseh and these demons. It's interesting that when James Dobson was invited to visit Ted Bundy on death row, a man who I believe was fatally possessed, he decided to go. Dr. Dobson would have prayed about this. When out of fear or legalism, we put limits on who can repent and be healed we place limits on God's mercy. There is a final door that closes in the life of every nonbeliever and for Ted Bundy that final door was very likely, Dr. James Dobson.

The prayer of Manasseh is not included in some Bibles. Since the Council of Trent it has been included as an appendix to the Latin Vulgate. I like this prayer because, in the words of this fallen king, we see the miracle of his turning to God via an act of faith. *Now faith is the assurance of things hoped for, the conviction of things not seen. For by it the men of old gained approval (Hebrews 11: 1, 2).* Manasseh confesses his many sins which were rooted in delusions, illusions, and incorrect beliefs cemented in a hedonistic lifestyle that preternaturally partnered with satan. Until he did an abrupt, about-face, he was a human conduit for evil.

Manasseh wrote his prayer in captivity, very far off from his former privileged and protected status, which had afforded him an uncensored lifestyle of debauchery. We sense the absolute astonishment he feels as he considers God's forgiveness, finding that in the face of major judgment delivered per the wrath of God; the scope of His wrath equals the immensity of His infinite grace and goodness.

Therefore the Lord brought the commanders of the army of the king of Assyria against them and they captured Manasseh with hooks, bound him with bronze chains and took him to Babylon (2nd Chronicles 33: 11).

During this captivity Manasseh had an opportunity to rethink his life. Maybe he remembered his father's love for God. Perhaps he was imprisoned in the company of someone who had memorized the writings of Moses and the law. In the powerful words of a repentant exile, this fallen and hated king who was corporately responsible for the suffering of his people and the fall of Judah wrote the following words.

...yet immeasurable and unsearchable is Your promised mercy, for You are the Lord Most High, of great compassion, long-suffering, and very merciful, and you relent at human suffering. O Lord, according to your great goodness you have promised repentance and forgiveness to those who have sinned against you, and in the multitude of your mercies you have appointed repentance for sinners, so that they may be saved (The Prayer of Manasseh: 6, 7). **Also Micah 7: 18; Ezekiel 36: 26, 27.**

God gave this humiliated and humbled, utterly disgraced king another chance. He restored the throne so that Manasseh could evidence the proof of this miraculous transformation of God's love in the fruit of willing obedience. How wonderful that Jesus shines a light into dark places, awareness of sin juxtaposed with His love and drawn to the miracle of immeasurable grace.

Read **2ⁿᵈ** *Chronicles 33: 10-17.* This reversal of judgment came about by one means. Manasseh says, *"I bend the knee of my heart."* I imagine him so fettered by hooks and chains that at this moment he could not physically kneel as he would like. In the words of a former satanically driven narcissist, in bondage to demonic alliances (hooks and chains; literal and spiritual) but reconciling to God, Manasseh writes: *And now I bend the knee of my heart, imploring You for Your kindness. I have sinned, O Lord, I have sinned, and I acknowledge my transgressions. I earnestly implore You, forgive me, O Lord, forgive me! Do not destroy me with my transgressions! Do not be angry with me forever or store up evil for me; do not condemn me to the depths of the earth. For You, O Lord, are the God of those who repent and in me you will manifest your goodness; for unworthy as I am, you will save me according to Your great mercy, and I will praise You continually all the days of my life. For all the host of heaven sings your praise; and yours is the glory forever. Amen. (The Prayer of Manasseh 11-15).*

I have an acquaintance who was heavily involved in multiple criminal activities before Jesus Christ found him. If I would say that he "came to Christ," he would correct me as he has others. He admits that growing up he was a handful. He rarely felt remorse over the pain he caused others. After returning from a "business" trip to his home in California he was taking a shower when he began to feel uncomfortable. Suddenly a veil lifted. He knew that God saw him. He said, *"I was mercy zapped."* This supernatural deluge of mercy drove him to his knees and he saw, for the first time in his life, sin juxtaposed with the love of Jesus Christ.

He said, *"It wasn't the fear of hell that drew me to God. I was so hardened that this was my identity and my fate. I thought all religious people were losers and judgmental and people like me had the upper hand, because we took it and made it happen. That was my philosophy of living. I didn't feel alive unless I was taking care of business and about that you don't want to know. But that was my drug of choice. God came to me and showed me that I was human on this hand and inhuman on this other hand and that inhuman part was consuming the part that God wanted to restore. His love was healing all of the person-me; naked flaws and all. Jesus let me know that He saw me and he had this compassion for how lost I was. That was it. I could cry. I feel such gratitude.*

*You could say I had a powerful religious experience. I had an expensive antique Buddha. I saw it as a good luck piece and I touched it every time I left the house. If I forgot and got out the gate I'd return no matter how late. It and other things, lots of spirits, had a grip on me and there was bondage; you don't want to know. I took a hammer to its base. A lot of time had gone by in that shower. I was dazed. The water was cold when I came out of it. I left the bathroom and after knocking it loose I rolled that idol and what it represented down the ravine behind my house. I just knew there wasn't going to be any room for my business and there wasn't going to be room for that Buddha. I found something else to do with the rest of my life and I was happy. Today I can't believe who and what I was. What happened to me was a miracle and if Jesus can happen to me in that way He can happen to anyone. That's what I believe with all my heart. I try to remember. **Is anything too difficult for the Lord? (Genesis 18: 14a).***

Not until we've recognized that our hurts and wounds are sadistically digested as fodder for the narcissistic supply, do we see the patterns of practice for what they are. Children raised by a narcissistic parent usually find themselves, at some point, in counseling wanting to understand these dynamics. Those that are Ambulatory Possessed, as Judas was, almost never show up asking for help.

Those who are Fatally Possessed are beyond help. They can't be saved and have committed the unpardonable sin described in **Mark 3: 27-30.**

Those engaged in deliverance and healing are informed in studying the many narcissistic characters in the Old and New Testament. Elijah ministered as prophet during the rule of Ahab and Jezebel. Ahab was a malevolent narcissist (ambulatory possessed). Jezebel was fatally possessed. It is not always God's will that we engage dangerous personalities. In **1ˢᵗ Kings 19**, after

106

Jezebel threatened his life, Elijah took the threat seriously. Her past behavior was an indicator of future behavior. Discerning context into behavior, juxtaposed with the will of God for that circumstance, Isaiah went into hiding. At other times it was necessary to engage peripherally or corporately. Read *1st Kings 18.*

What should be noted is that no prophet ever engaged Jezebel head-on. This is because, by the time we meet her, she is fatally possessed. *Do not give what is holy to dogs, and do not throw your pearls before swine, or they will trample them under feet, and turn and tear you to pieces (Matthew 7: 6).*

Only recently, in the late sixties and early seventies, was Narcissistic Personality Disorder defined as a spectrum disorder. The clinical research on narcissism came about as more adult children raised by narcissistic parents presented for treatment. As seeking treatment became socially acceptable, smart psychologists began to recognize that they could not help these patients without understanding commonalities associated with the perpetrator caretaker. These changes dropped into greater awareness and naturally merged with what was known of psychopaths and chronic criminal behavior. It is said that less than one percent of the population suffer with malignant narcissism. I personally think this is far higher and needs to be more broadly understood as having a preternatural imprint and influence. Because there is so much bias within the profession against using religious terms the obvious connections are slow to come.

D. Corydon Hammond, Ph.D. gave a very brave and singular speech which blew the lid of secrecy and containment off a very explosive topic. Originally titled: *Hypnosis in MPD: Ritual Abuse,* his presentation is now more commonly known as, **The Greenbaum Speech**. He said what many others thought, but didn't have the courage to state; that there was a growing incidence and stark correlation between Dissociative Disorder and Satanic Ritual Abuse. Tapes from other lectures from this very conference are still available, but not Dr. Hammond's lecture which was delivered on June 25, 1992 to a room full of doctors interested in Multiple Personality Disorder, now called Dissociative Disorder.

Since giving this talk, Dr. Hammond, who is Mormon, has distanced himself from what he shared on that day. His abrupt and sudden silence speaks volumes about an area that the Christian community and law enforcement need to stop enabling via silence and constrained reporting and investigation. This is no surprise to Ken Thornberg of Freedom Encounters, who at the time of Hammonds' speech, was already working with the integration of alters in deliverance. You can find Dr. Hammond's lecture on-line and read. Ken Thornberg has spent over twenty five years working with victims of Satanic Ritual Abuse (SRA). He has consulted with medical professionals and law enforcement. His work is a beacon of light out of bondage and he has spent many years training others to practice deliverance.

I've been asked if people with mental illness are demon possessed and the question itself always feels half stupid and half trick. Demons camp on any weakness or illness when they've been given legal access. Forms of most mental illness are physical disorders of the brain. Healing may manifest as a sudden and complete miracle or it may be a process that involves medical treatment. *Healing* by, Francis MacNutt is a balanced and insightful book.

Nina Haines wrote a book called, *Flying Backwards.* This honest account tells the story of Nina and Mark Haines's son, Jon, who suffered from a type of schizophrenia which first manifested in childhood. The book tells Jon's personal struggle. Nina chronicles how mental illness impacted the family, explores the response of the Christian community, how she and Mark retained a strong faith and worked through the stresses that impacted their marriage. She shares how they navigated the mental health system while supporting Jon throughout his short life.

Nina and Mark never stopped praying and believing that God would physically heal Jon. There were times when they prayed against demonic influence. Nina recognized the danger of Jon harming, himself or others and knew that in his "right mind" this would not be his choice. She learned to pray deliverance for Jon in ways that were not a trigger for his illness. In her book she offers a balanced and practical approach, understanding that within the constructs of mental illness as a brain disorder and informed by her faith, Jon was both protected and vulnerable. Jon Haines left us for heaven at age twenty-four as he faced another cycling relapse into psychosis. God allowed both his parents an after death impartation that assured them that Jon was in heaven with His savior, Jesus Christ. In a dream Jon said to his father, "It's beautiful here." To His mother Jesus said, "I have him, Nina."

It's helpful to read personal stories of those impacted by narcissistic personalities as children, spouses, or cult entrapment. It's also important to understand the rise of false prophets and cults as heralding the start of the Revelation events and the return of Jesus Christ. History, viewed through the Judeo-Christian lens points to this being the case prior to every significant correction.

Believers need to identify narcissistic traits evidencing in church leadership. We must gird ourselves to recognize emerging toxic and dangerous cult leaders, dictators, and political leaders who endanger our existence. The Antichrist of end times will be a fatally possessed malevolent narcissist. Scripture tells us that his true heart will be concealed by the deluding power of demonic spirits juxtaposed in a dynamic personality which will deceive the masses. *For this reason God will send upon them a deluding influence so that they will believe what is false (2nd Thessalonians 2: 11).*

This last antichrist figure will seize power during a world crisis as a springboard to world domination. He'll be the antithesis of all that Christ was. The Father sent His Son into the world as a helpless babe, into poor and humble circumstances, but this last antichrist figure will come from great wealth and privilege. *Isaiah: 53.*

The son of perdition may even have ties to an earthy royal household. By the time he comes to power he'll already evidence a strong preternaturally controlled persona and will have been strategically positioned for what occult mages mistakenly interpret from Revelation. Most Satanists are knowledgeable about end-times prophecy. The difference is that they are so deluded as to prescribe a different outcome or rendition of future events. Although it won't be immediately obvious, the antichrist will have a profound disdain for women, common in all fatally possessed vehicles and indelibly stamped into pagan terrorist cultures.

The world over, when significant crisis hits, untold numbers will be primed to worship this figure as an idol; fascinated with his status, appearance, influence, and charisma. This final antichrist will show no loyalty to any other demon; nor to any loyal cult follower. All those demons worshipped by his family tree throughout the ages will mean nothing to him. *Then the king will do as he pleases, and he will exalt and magnify himself above every god and will speak monstrous things against the God of gods, and he will prosper until the indignation is finished, for that which is decreed will be done. He will show no regard for the gods of his fathers' or for the desire of women, nor will he show regard for any other god; for he will magnify himself above them all (Daniel 11: 36, 37).* This future king of coming judgment will be fatally possessed by satan. By this time satan will no longer have access to heaven and will take over the body of this, currently unknown man.

I consciously write three roles into fiction. I also use these labels which I assign to people in the investigative stage of deliverance. These are: *The Perpetrator, The Passive Facilitator,* and lastly *The Caustic Agent for Change.* In life and fiction these roles overlap.

For example the character of the judge in *Wood's End* who finally does turn to Christ has played all three roles. We feel outrage at the perpetrator, frustration and loss of respect for the passive facilitator, and sympathy for the child victim he once was. The police detective, even before he trusts Christ, is a moral person who plays the role of the caustic agent for change. Only after he turns to Christ for salvation is the character of Jared supernaturally empowered to banish evil from having sway and influence. Think about these labels and how they inform the roles that people have played in your life.

Passive facilitators may have started out as victims, but if they do not extricate themselves via God-given tools of autonomy and choice they move from victim to volunteer. Now they are part of the problem; failing to speak up and act up. The perpetrator-narcissist carefully selects and grooms vulnerable people to fill this role. We see this dynamic in all evil circumstances, agenda's, and outcomes. With flat affect or false joviality, via delusional fields of blindness and parroting articulate renditions of a lie, volunteers move into being every bit as guilty.

In Jennifer's account of what she suffered her step-father was the obvious perpetrator. The grandmother who failed to report Jennifer's account of sexual abuse became a passive facilitator, partnering with evil. The moment she decided to turn a blind eye, failing to rescue Jennifer, she became a perpetrator, voluntarily and preternaturally enmeshed to the demonically controlled pedophile. The mother, turning her God-given autonomy and parental authority over to a pedophile opted for blindness. She was also a passive facilitator. We can see how the pedophile step father would have selected and then arranged and manipulated the family dynamics in order to continue his abuse of his narcissistic supply-- the child, Jennifer. We also recognize the satanic death-agenda. And now we see the stronghold.

It is often because we first identify the facilitating volunteers and then recognize the degree of enmeshed partnership, that we are finally led to the perpetrator who may be quite adept at hiding and shifting blame.

The caustic agent for change is the salt and light that all Christians are commanded to risk. Not a passive faith, but a radical stalwart faith. **Read Acts chapters 6 and 7**. When Stephen spoke truth to power he lost his life. Some have lost jobs or position, been maligned and ridiculed, asked to leave their churches and alienated family. Others, all across this world in ever growing numbers, are being martyred for their faith.

And they overcame him because of the blood of the

Lamb and because of the word of their testimony, and they did not love their life even when faced with death (Revelation 12: 11).

CHAPTER ELEVEN

FOUR MOVIES – HOMEWORK DISGUISED AS ENTERTAINMENT

Many books and movies include narcissism as a theme. I personally think that most highly creative people have been impacted by narcissistic caretakers and perpetrators. We spend a life time working out the dynamics of having navigated the contradictions and confusion of being at the mercy of such people during the formative years of life. For some, the arts become a way to understand what happened to us before words were learned to frame the experience of such satanic exposure.

Here is a homework assignment. Watch four movies. Be entertained, but also write your thoughts about the characters and the roles they play in being perpetrators, passive facilitators, and caustic agents for change. The movies are: *White Oleander, Spanglish, Suddenly Last Summer,* and one of my all time favorites, *Gosford Park.*

Refer back to Scott Peck's description of evil behavior in the last chapter understanding that all these traits need to be present. As you watch these films check off examples of these traits and strategies at work in a consistent basis via the plot and evidenced in the characters patterns of practice. Begin to develop a protocol of recognition. Via deliberate and strategic tools of observation step into honing your "discerning spirits" gift as a specific skill set. You've decided to embrace and grow this skill set so that you can sharpen the eyes of the heart to recognize good and evil in service to the kingdom of God.

In *Gosford Park*, written by the very brilliant, Julian Fellowes, the Lord of the Manor is a serial rapist with psychopathic features. He is either ambulatory or fatally possessed. I'd vote for the later. At no time do we see any evidence of conscience or kindness. There is no faculty of self awareness which operates to check his behavior. Wealth has insulated him and he has learned from life that if he plays his cards right and retains a certain status the rules he already believes don't apply to him, actually don't. William McCordle, played by, Michael Gambon, is hypersensitive to criticism, and totally focused on protecting his criminal behavior. This character is surrounded by so many passive facilitators that we are hard pressed to name them all, but try, writing down the many missed opportunities.

The caustic agent for change in this film is very obviously the cook, Mrs. Croft. Played by Eileen Atkins, this character fully understands who she is working for. Who else plays this role? Some step in and out of the passive-facilitator-volunteer role. Who are they?

There is another narcissistic perpetrator in this film. The parallels between the two allow us a glimpse into the opportunistic features which mature and become more sophisticated as a criminal learns to self protect life stealing, addictive sin. This was a clever turn of writing to show the younger, Henry Denton character informed by the William McCordle behavior and the similarities between the younger and the older man.

There is no true deliverance from evil without first identifying the unseen preternatural partnerships which need to be cast off, sent to Jesus Christ for immediate judgment and then consigned to the abyss never to be heard from again and with all backups and replacements also destroyed. For both these men there would be a root, a beginning wound, a first series of decisions that set up the patterns of practice to operate under satanic assignment. On the other hand there may be no social-psycho cause and effect and we do not need, nor will we ever, know everything. In this movie the script hints at what may have gone wrong for both men. Consider that in the blind pursuit of ambition, although Henry Denton is not homosexual, he uses his sexuality as an impersonal tool of contrivance which at each step is subjugating the human under the auspices of the inhuman. Note the subtle body language as he makes an excuse not to have sexual relationship with the producer as he stands by the fire place in the bedroom. We feel compassion for this character since he can be healed and restored if he would turn to Christ.

The movies *White Oleander* and *Spanglish* show a malevolent narcissist and a full blown narcissist in the lead roles. Even before psychologists were tracking this disorder those of us who have been impacted by them down through the ages have been compelled to draw creatively from them. Shakespeare is one example. Time and time again we are drawn to his work because we recognize the true depiction of evil personified in the complicated flux and angst of life. We see too that all people can have their evil moments, but can reverse course and strive for healing; adopting profound change. There are examples of this in the films I'm asking you to watch, but I particularly want you to see and make no excuse for the demonically controlled narcissists.

It's interesting that in *Spanglish*, the Deborah character mentions narcissism in association with her behavior, but only as a manipulative tool to stop the thought process that could take her husband down the road toward dealing with and actually confronting her chronic narcissistic (hurtful and life-stealing) behavior. Notice her striking body language in this dramatic moment.

The passive facilitators in these films should be clear. The attorney who supports the Michelle Pfeiffer character in manipulating the daughter to testify and lie on her mother's behalf allows the mother character, as a skilled narcissistic manipulator, to extend her reach while incarcerated for murder.

In the film *Spanglish* both the husband, played so well by Adam Sandler, and Deborah's alcoholic mother act out these facilitator roles. Sadly the father is teaching his beloved daughter, Bernie, to accept what she should reject and thus we see how satan is given legal access to infect future generations. At times the writing is quite subtle, but the father is very much a passive facilitator.

We additionally see this handing down of demonic imprints to the next generation in the daughter character, Isobel, in *Gosford Park* who has had an abortion. She has been attracted to the familiar narcissistic characteristics of her father in the choice of the man she has given herself to; an opportunistic predator, who cannot marry her and will never love her. When you watch this film, note the alert observance of the Mabel Nesbitt character. Not much of the subtext escapes this woman and she very likely has a gift for discerning spirits. We almost have a little hope for her husband as she stands up to him, refusing to adopt his morals and standards as her own. This was developed a little more in the outtakes that did not make it into the film.

In working out her conflicts with her mother, sweet Bernie will likely be drawn to marry a man who is very much like Deborah and especially because her father has not defended innocence and her fragile sensibilities as he should. We like him for trying, but does he go far enough? I felt a lot of compassion for the daughters in these three films and additionally for Henry Denton and how his life might have been different with early intervention. A character in the film holds up a mirror to Henry. He has been socialized and conditioned so as not to recognize his predatory actions as sin. Discuss this scene and what it means, the similarities implied in how both men have unhealed trauma in their lives from which they need deliverance.

As our world grows more evil, and the tools of warfare shift in a changing culture, becoming more sophisticated, we need to stop living in fantasy land as volunteer-perpetrators and passive facilitators who posture a superficial, neutered faith with no power to change anything.

What I especially like about the writing and directing of *White Oleander* is what can be understood about the daughter's journey to free herself as a victim of a narcissistic parent. In the *Spanglish* film I like the visual and contextual example of the maid who has yet to learn English and yet is very discerning in her ability to read her employer (Deborah's) behavior. Flor reads the subtext, discerns the spirits of her employer and is drawn to very specific conclusions which become the moral impetus to disengage from the dysfunction in order to protect herself and her child. And in the end, she disengages from both the perpetrator and the passive facilitator. Good writing.

In all these films we are provided an insightful glimpse into the fierce and prevalent need for perpetrators to maintain a ready narcissistic supply of victims. In *Spanglish*, as the husband emotionally withdraws, Deborah, who has no tolerance for the shelf position in life, first has an affair and then attaches herself to Flor's daughter. Like all predators she is ready to take advantage of any imbalance of power. There are at least five other instances that Deborah evidences this behavior. Recognize them and write them down.

In the practice of discerning spirits you are learning to identify the subtle nuances of a script that reveals truth. These keys are the language of spiritual understanding. These clues reveal what hides behind the delusional façade; the imprint, infestation, and influence. The more you submit to the Holy Spirit in this practice and the more deliberate becomes the process, the more skilled you will become; allowing God to train and empower such a gift.

Deborah's need for a consistent narcissistic supply to feed her dis-ease is vividly portrayed as she returns home after a daylong outing where she has pampered and entertained the maid's daughter. We notice that she offers nothing like this to her own daughter. Although not fully developed, the Deborah character would have felt entitled to a physically beautiful daughter and yet as this daughter grew up she would have jealously guarded herself as the center of attention, not tolerating any competition. Bernie's good and gracious heart, all her sensitivity and generosity, are not recognized assets. Not in Deborah's superficial world.

As the writer develops this character we see that Deborah has taken Flor's daughter (Christina) off with no explanation and without her permission which throws the house in an uproar. With young exuberance Christina tries to express her admiration and appreciation of Deborah's attention. Overwhelmed with gratitude Christina is at a loss for words. Deborah prompts, "No, tell me," guiding the narcissistic supply (Christina) to stroke the bottomless pit of an exaggerated self interest and with no self awareness of the chaos and worry left in the wake of her behavior.

Narcissists do not comprehend the notion of boundaries and if they do they see them as obstacles that must be breached in order to gain an ever more intrusive and lethal access to the narcissistic supply. The narcissist takes advantage of any perceived imbalance of power and has a developed antenna to do so. The feelings and offended sensibilities of those they hurt are no more than an irritant. If confronted and forced to see their behavior for what it is, they become dangerous, cornered wolves, hyper sensitive to criticism. Others have adopted a victim shield of defense. They'll punish all who confront them with the threat of physical suffering; "poor me."

Another film which powerfully demonstrates narcissism to the extreme is *Suddenly Last Summer*. This film is important because it shows the enmeshed relationship between the narcissist (the mother) and her narcissistic supply (her recently deceased son.) At times it almost feels like Katherine Hepburn is overacting. But in truth, she is doing an excellent job of portraying the partnered demonic withdrawal from the narcissistic supply; which is intensely emotional, personal, and physical.

It is at these junctures of intense grief and loss (rage), that we can minister Christ to these people. They are confronting the finality of death or forced to face consequences. Some "thing" is beyond their reach and influence. This threatens the magical thinking associated with all demonically erected strongholds. They can hardly let go of the notion that they should have been, were entitled to, orchestrate a different outcome. As change agents and Holy Spirit carriers we can offer the only solution, Jesus Christ. Or at the very least, we can plant seeds and perhaps rejoice in a Manasseh outcome.

Violet Venable, played by Katherine Hepburn, enables the pedophile son and attempts to lobotomize the one person who can dismantle her satanically deluded constructs of an idol; the revered and perfect son, her possession. Her absolute belief that it is her duty and her right to control the thoughts and conclusions of other people, that she has such power at her disposal to rewrite history, becomes an obsession. This is a common trait of narcissists. Later in life many have returned to confront a narcissistic, demonically possessed parent only to find that they will receive no justice related to any admission of wrong doing. Not in this life time.

A question to ask as we move beyond the idea that these characters suffer from Narcissistic Personality Disorder is this. What is, and how enmeshed are, the demonic attachments with the core personality? None are conflicted possessed since they are all operational. Can you make a case for any being Ambulatory

Possessed or Fatally Possessed?

If your plan is to step into a Deliverance Ministry where investigation, counseling partnerships, and aftercare is provided you'll need to have some God-given skill for drawing certain conclusions. Godly discernment as a spiritual gift will need to be present. You'll also find yourself primarily working with the victims of these dangerous people who are desperately in need of healing and freedom in Jesus Christ from the curses such proximity builds into the victims. Many are physically ill or have besetting sins and addictions, but they are only superficially being helped if a spiritual answer through faith is not being offered. Many are also in the church. You pass them in the hall going here or there. Reach out and look for those that may need what God designed your spiritual gift set to offer via a miracle of His grace.

As you watch *Suddenly Last Summer*, notice that Violet's niece, Catherine, played by Elizabeth Taylor, threatens to dismantle the magical thought-stronghold; the story, the alligator farm. For Violet, a psychotic break is entirely possible at such times and we begin to see that Violet can so easily unravel. This plot introduces her as self sufficient and capable, but we soon see the satanic imprint left in the wake of her behavior. What Violet needs is a caustic agent for change, a Holy Spirit carrier who will offer deliverance and share the only hope of healing; Jesus Christ. Is she beyond help?

Violet Venable has only worshipful admiration; seeing her deceased son as her god-like creation. As he grew from child to man this mother groomed her son to be the narcissistic supply until he stepped over the line to volunteer and then, to be an even greater diabolical perpetrator. Note the location of his cottage. Notice his attempted replacement of the mother with his younger, more beautiful cousin and the addictive, life stealing compulsions that made this replacement necessary.

As the doctor begins to evaluate Violet's insistence that Catherine be lobotomized, we see the doctor slowly breaking through the satanic, delusional field of energy to get at buried truth. At first confused, befuddled and wishing to reject the evidence, he comes to identify Violet as the perpetrator. Notice the similar expressions on the faces of this doctor and the maid in the film *Spanglish,* as they both move forward in reading the subtext of the behavior, the language so very at odds with their own moral compass. Although his education has not prepared the doctor to take this further into the spiritual realm of warfare, what scripture teaches, and the tools provided via faith we see him putting the pieces together as a very effective caustic agent for change. Because of his willingness to do this work, to take a stand for truth and justice, Catherine is saved.

Narcissists have been called soulless. I think of them as being empty shelled; empty vehicles; already the perfect conduit for demonic possession. Devoid of empathy, lacking the genuine compassion that marks them as life giving and nourishing, they lack a human compass and are in constant need of a *narcissistic supply*.

What should be our response for those who practice life-stealing compulsions as desperately as any addict needing a fix? ***...save others by snatching them out of the fire; and have mercy on still others with fear, hating even the tunic defiled by their bodies (Jude 23).***

Why wouldn't a compassionate God equip some believers to discern these spirits? He did and He has.

Those that have lived for any length of time around toxic and narcissistic personalities may have by transference demonic attachments which they need healing and deliverance from. A symptom of those who need deliverance is that they have no joy and at heart believe many negative lies. They have saving faith, but need freedom to embrace the fullness of God's word through healing and deliverance. ***And to know the love of Christ, which passes knowledge, that ye might be filled with all the fullness of God (Ephesians 3: 19).***

Make a little popcorn and prepare to watch and make notes about the characters in these films. I recommend you watch them more than once and perhaps even form a discussion group. See how all the narcissistic and dangerous personalities in these films have attractive features. Others are charming and amusing and draw us into the sphere of influence as Deborah does. Violet attempts to bribe those she seeks to manipulate in buying her story. She invites them to turn a blind eye and hands over the rationale for doing so in the form of a story; a complete package telling others what to think, feel, and do.

A few of these characters act out the dynamics of redeeming moments, the façade that lulls us into thinking these perpetrators will change and grow. We want the best for them; we want to think they can behave to better standards. Sorry, they won't and they can't. Not without a miracle of deliverance, healing and restoration. Not without Jesus Christ.

THE END

***But if I cast out demons by the finger of God,
then the kingdom of God has come upon you. Luke 11: 20***

YOUR NOTES

Made in the USA
Charleston, SC
28 September 2013